the **strategy**
activation
playbook

A Practical Approach to
Bringing Your Strategies to Life

ARIC WOOD
+ XPLANE

Matt Holt is an imprint of BenBella Books, Inc.
10440 N. Central Expressway
Suite 800
Dallas, TX 75231
benbellabooks.com
Send feedback to feedback@benbellabooks.com

BenBella and *Matt Holt* are federally registered trademarks.

Printed in the United States of America
10 9 8 7 6 5 4 3 2 1

Library of Congress Control Number: 2022935035
ISBN 9781637741825 (trade paperback)
ISBN 9781637741832 (electronic)

Editing by Katie Dickman
Proofreading by Jenny Bridges and Cape Cod Compositors, Inc.
Indexing by WordCo Indexing Services
Layout and page design by Nicole Bittner
Illustration and design by Jeffery Frankenhauser, Tim May, Catie Cooper
Cover design by Tim May and Jeffery Frankenhauser
Printed by Versa Press

Special discounts for bulk sales are available. Please contact bulkorders@benbellabooks.com.

For Hadius

Humans will eventually manifest
that which they imagine.

contents

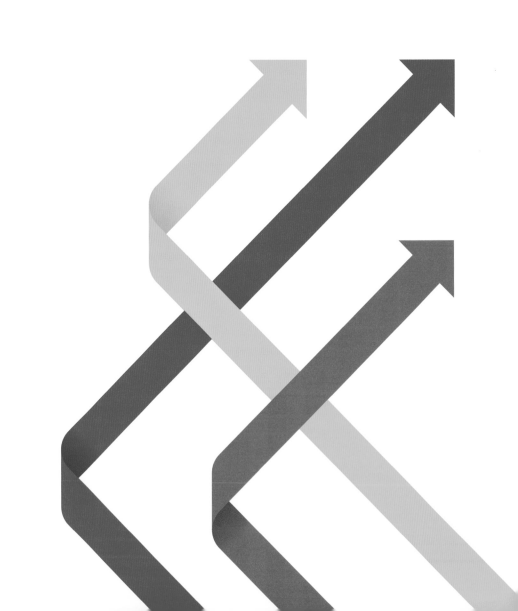

introduction

Strategy activation is an emerging field. Not quite change management, definitely not strategy execution, strategy activation is a new discipline emerging in tandem with the modern organization, which is more diverse, empowered, and independent-minded than the top-down, hierarchical organizations of old.

Strategy activation fits in between strategic planning and strategy execution. The space between these two is the desert where strategy goes to die.

Brought up in old models of business, many leaders still believe that when we jump directly from strategic plans to strategy execution people will just follow along. But that's not our current reality. Because organizations now compete on creativity and innovation, we have built a creative and empowered workforce which thinks for themselves. And in

that gap between strategic planning and strategy execution, there is a choice. These empowered, critically-thinking teams can decide for themselves whether they agree with the strategy and the plan—and whether they plan to follow it.

Strategy activation, and change activation at large, is about understanding the people in the system: their wants, needs, and barriers to change, and how to persuade them to join your cause and move forward together. It's about bridging that gap between strategic planning and strategy execution with a new, critical middle ground that persuades, aligns, and engages people to move in new directions.

As such, it's a new branch within the realm of business acumen—anchored not in the typical MBA curriculum but more in psychology, learning and development theory, and design thinking (with its tenets of empathy, observation,

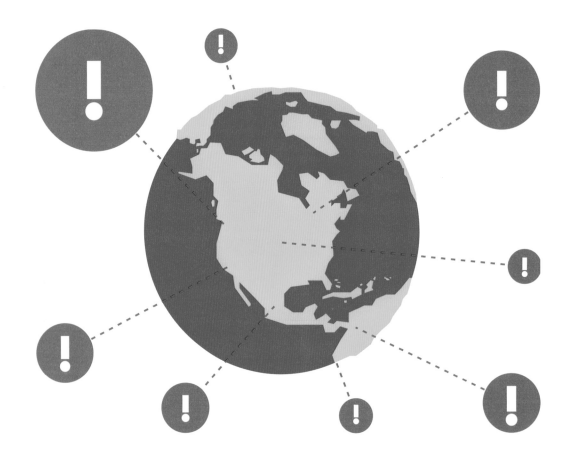

and user-centricity). It requires upgrading current systems of business and change management with a new toolkit of capabilities and methods drawn from broad disciplines, far afield from traditional business training.

As the world changes, and the pace of change only continues to accelerate, a leader's ability to navigate change while motivating people to achieve an organization's purpose will be one of the most important new capabilities to nurture, and is critical to leadership success.

Based on three decades of experience leading strategy activation programs across the spectrum of organizations from Fortune 500 to government entities, global NGOs, and nonprofit organizations of all sizes, we've assembled a successful framework, a toolkit of methods, and a set of proven principles and best practices, which collectively shape the emerging practice of strategy activation.

This book is a playbook for leaders to activate change—a toolkit you can begin to apply immediately in developing your own organization's capacity to change and adopt new strategies at scale.

part 1
why strategies fail

In most organizations, strategies are dead before they are launched.

We've all seen this show: the organization brings together leaders to develop a new strategy, or outsources the work to a strategy consulting firm, and the result is a 150-page PowerPoint presentation that's incomprehensible to all but the authors. The strategy then gets unveiled by the CEO at a Town Hall meeting, after which every employee is expected to understand their role and begin executing the plan.

But that's not what happens. We know from research that 80 percent of strategies fail,[1] despite an incredible initial investment in strategy development. It's estimated that organizations spend over $160 billion globally to hire outside consultants[2]—and likely many multiples of that, when you consider the internal time and expense of strategy development and execution, as well as the hard-cost investments required to support the strategy itself.

This is an incredible black hole of waste, and a significant drain on an organization's ability to compete and advance their mission. With an 80 percent failure rate, the return on investment for strategy work is abysmal, and yet we continue to see the strategy consulting industry growing year after year.

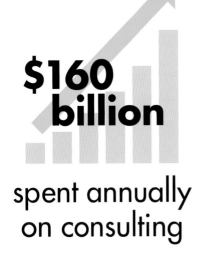

$160 billion

spent annually on consulting

80%

of strategies **fail**

Importantly, this phenomenon isn't only true of global corporate strategies, but all types of strategies across the organization—from enterprise-wide shifts to functional process changes, culture transformations, and new approaches to working at every level. Any change that requires people to do something differently than the way they have worked historically may be considered a strategy shift, subject to the same investment in shifting people's mindsets, behaviors, and ways of working.

It's time to examine what's happening here, and how we can fix it. So, why do strategies fail, and how can you as a leader beat the odds?

Many studies have looked at this question, and of course the answer is complex. There may be competitive and external factors resulting in unforeseen circumstances that undermine the strategy. Perhaps the strategy doesn't consider or overestimates the actual capabilities of the organization. It's possible that the strategy itself is flawed.

However, if we net these factors out, and focus on the people side of the equation, the picture becomes clearer. In our thirty years of working with global firms doing strategy activation work, we've seen that strategies fail for three primary reasons.

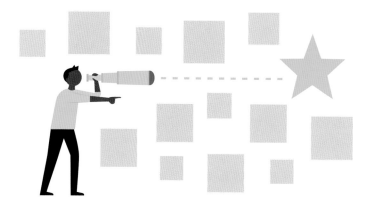

First: Employee Line of Sight

Our biggest failing is that we treat organizations like a machine that can be programmed: if we point in a new direction, we expect the organization to go there. But organizations are made up of people, each with their own mind, wants, and needs. As a result, each person needs to understand not only what we're doing and why, but also—very importantly—what their role is. They need to understand where they fit in, how they contribute, and how their work has meaning.

We call this line of sight: the ability to see clearly how one's role and responsibilities ladder up to support the larger strategy.

Most organizations are terrible at deploying strategy at this level. Organizations typically paint a reasonably clear view of where they want the entire organization to go, but they usually fail to address how the strategy will impact different stakeholders in the organization—and to bring it to life for the very employees that must carry it forward.

Second: Lack of Employee Engagement

The second reason strategies fail is that we often ignore the importance of employee engagement. Employees need to see clearly how they are linked to the strategy (line of sight). And to move to action, they must also have an emotional connection to the organization and its goals, along with some participation in the process. People want to connect to a greater purpose and to understand how what they do contributes to it.

And yet, employees are rarely engaged in strategy development, and often not even in the planning for strategy execution. It's part of the reason consultants get the bad rap of just throwing a plan over the wall. But they aren't wholly to blame: leaders of the organization need to find ways to

engage employees at key points throughout the process to surface their insights and engage them in planning and execution.

Even if an employee sees the path forward clearly, to join you they need to want to embark on the journey. For them to do that, they need to clearly understand the why of the change, what's in it for them, how they will be supported, and, most importantly, how they can contribute.

Engaging employees in the process not only brings their valuable insights into the strategy and action plan, but it also accelerates adoption, because they feel some ownership of the result.

Third: Lack of Investment in Activation

Finally, the largest reason strategies fail is that we simply don't plan and resource an activation program that engages our teams to bring the strategies we create to life. We plan a plan, but we don't plan how to engage people in the plan.

Imagine designing a house with an architect, creating a blueprint design, sourcing the site and materials, and then expecting all the contractors to just show up and magically collaborate to build the structure. We'd never do that—instead, we'd sit down with a general contractor and architect to develop a detailed plan to build our house in a phased approach, with clear roles and responsibilities for who does what, when, and in what order, to ensure that our vision for the house becomes real, and it's built as we expect.

And yet, with many strategies, we hire the architect (strategy consultants) to design detailed strategic plans but make very little, if any, investment in planning *how* we'll bring those plans to life. We share the blueprint, but we don't take the

next, critical steps to organize our teams and equip them for success.

There are numerous, well-researched studies that outline other points of failure in strategy execution, and it's not our intent to dismiss them—we can learn something from all of them. However, as it relates to the people side of the equation, which is this book's focus, these three failure points are the most common ones we've seen in our work. We'll explore each in the next chapters.

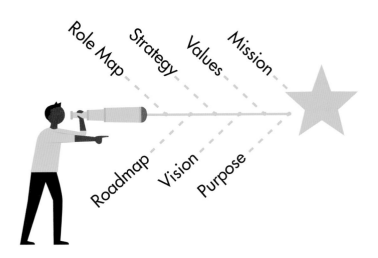

Line of Sight

We defined line of sight as the ability to see clearly how a person's role and responsibilities ladder up to and support the larger strategy.

I said that most organizations are terrible at deploying strategy at this level, leading to a failure to truly bring it to life for the very employees that must carry it forward. What I mean by that is this: The best organizations are often very good at socializing their mission, purpose, values, vision, even their strategy. These elements are all shared anchors that are (or should be) consistent across the organization, regardless of where you sit within it.

But even the best organizations often fail to go to the next step: linking these shared anchors to individual roadmaps of teams and roles of individuals. This is the critical "last mile" in generating line of sight.

To visualize this, we call the sum of these elements your organization's navigation system. Your navigation system is the combination of anchor elements that allow an employee to clearly understand the organization's reason for being, its culture, its plans, and their role within it. It often looks like this: mission, purpose, values, vision, strategy, roadmap, and role map.

We'll delve into the navigation system later in the book, but for now, it should be apparent that each element of the system needs to be aligned and linked. Our vision should show us what our future looks like as we pursue our purpose and mission. Our values should describe how we behave in the pursuit of our vision. Our strategy should describe our plan to achieve our vision, and so on.

To create line of sight, we need to link up the navigation system completely for each employee. Most often, the critical points of connection are the next steps between the strategy, the roadmap, and each individual's role map.

The roadmap breaks the strategy down into achievable parts. Not everyone on the team will go to the summit: some will supply the team, some will row the boat, some will build the base camp. Having a clear roadmap that links teams to their roles in the strategy is a key next step.

Each employee should then have a clear sense of their role in the strategy. The role map, in whatever format your organization employs, should make clear what part of the strategy roadmap each person contributes to and their unique role within it.

The antidote to the problem of lack of line of sight is closing that gap and mapping the "last mile" for each employee or stakeholder. It requires an investment in "sensemaking" for each unique function, team, and individual to help them see what the roadmap of implementation is and what their unique part or contribution will be.

Only then can people achieve line of sight between themselves and the organization's larger goals. Each individual must understand clearly what the bigger picture is and be able to define how the work they do is meaningful to achieving the larger mission. This breeds increased alignment and engagement, which translates into better individual performance and faster organizational momentum.

There's a well-known story of the custodian at NASA headquarters in Houston in 1961, when President Kennedy visited. Asked what he did, the custodian replied "I'm here to help put a man on the moon." That man had clear line of sight between his role and the larger mission of the organization.

Employee Engagement

We defined employee engagement as having an emotional connection to the organization and its goals. Writ large, every organization must invest to ensure that employees feel aligned and emotionally connected to the organization and its navigation system. It takes a conscious effort to build that connection and an authentic commitment to maintaining and growing those connections over time.

Any time we launch a new strategy of any kind, the same will be true for that strategy: we need to invest to ensure that employees feel an emotional connection to the what, why, and how of this new direction, and an investment in the process of bringing it to life.

If developing line of sight makes clear each employee's role in the journey and a vision of the destination, the investment in employee engagement is one we must make for them to want to embark on the journey. They must feel an emotional connection to the goal and want to help move the organization forward to that place.

So, the antidote to a lack of employee engagement is to invest in helping employees clearly understand the why of the change, what's in it for them, how they will be supported, how they can contribute, and the reward at the end.

To do this, we need to develop our empathy skills. We need to understand each stakeholder's wants, needs, fears, and potential barriers to change, and how to address those as quickly as possible in order to accelerate their engagement in the change.

We also want to engage them in the change itself by honoring their knowledge, expertise, and good ideas through active involvement in the journey. People feel more engaged and excited about changes they have had a hand in creating, and the very act of co-creating details of the journey with participants will both result in a better plan and engage the participants in seeing it through successfully.

Consultants get a bad rap because they are perceived as seeing themselves as "the smartest person in the room" and as throwing solutions over the wall into the organization. Whether this is real or not, this perception is a strategy-killer for a number of reasons.

First, that the perception breeds distrust. The idea of outsiders coming in to tell people their own business never engenders trust and engagement. People develop expertise in their roles and functions, feel ownership of those areas, and are threatened by or at least dismissive of external experts who don't engage them and honor their expertise.

Second, the people in the organization do, in fact, possess insights that must be considered for an understanding of the business context, with potential gaps and opportunities that may make a strategy more or less effective. No one expert, even internal leaders, can possibly see the entire picture— and these blind spots can sink a strategy at the point of execution.

And lastly, the perception doesn't allow room for ownership. People support that which they help to build, but the opposite is true when they haven't been engaged. Without a sense of ownership, people tend to be indifferent to or even hostile to solutions that they didn't have a hand in creating.

Hence, employee engagement in the strategy process is a powerful antidote. We have a saying at XPLANE that the smartest person in the room IS the room, meaning that any idea can be made better by engaging a broad group of people in the process, especially those responsible for implementing the solution.

Whether in the making of the strategy itself or in the details of its execution, actively engaging employees yields better insights and engenders a sense of shared ownership that will accelerate adoption over time.

"

The smartest person in the room IS the room.

"

Investment in Activation

Investing in activation simply means that once we have a new strategy, which we can think of as a design, we also create a plan to bring that design to life.

Remember the example of designing a house with an architect. It just makes sense that once the design is done, we'd plan out how to coordinate all the people needed to build the structure. Each person needs to understand the bigger picture and the end goal, of course. But they also need to understand what's in it for them, what role they have to play, how they'll be supported with resources to do their job, and how and when they need to coordinate with others.

Sadly, very few organizations build this planning phase into their strategy development process. In most cases, there is a detailed strategic planning process that is conducted either in house or with external partners, but once the plan is developed it's rarely supported with an equally well-considered activation program. More often, it's simply expected that the plan will be cascaded through the ranks, and the organization will move rapidly from strategy planning to strategy execution.

So it should be no surprise that most of these strategies are dead before they begin. In what other area of our lives do we see examples where plans magically come to life without defining the steps to move from design to build to realization— and then actually taking those actions? In fact, in most areas of our lives, more energy is spent after a plan is created than in making the plan itself.

Let's look to some parallel examples. We already talked about building a house. What about making a film? The script could be the strategy, but then there's the effort of pitching, financing, casting, costuming, direction, editing, etc. In product design, the heavier investment might be in prototyping, materials sourcing, manufacturing, distribution, marketing, and so on. What about that moonshot? Kennedy's vision and strategy was clearly stated: "This nation should commit itself to achieving the goal, before the decade is out, of landing a man on the moon and returning him safely to the Earth." But executing the strategy required enormous investments in communications, training, and technology, along with the coordination of huge networks of people.

You get the idea. In every case, in terms of energy, the effort is significantly weighted in terms of what happens after the plan, not before. Well, of course, you may say, but surely organizations make similar investments in technology and the like to bring a strategy to life? That might be true of hard-cost investments, like technology and staffing, but it's just not so when it comes to the investment required in the coordination of people.

Recall we said that $160 billion a year was spent on consulting? According to a recent report by BCG, change management consulting is a $10 billion industry,[3] which suggests that the people part of this change work is about 6 percent of our total investment in strategy making and execution.

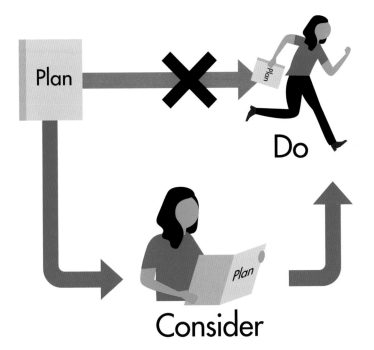

So why do we fail to properly invest in activating business strategies? Bottom line, we're working under an old set of assumptions: we still believe that organizations are top-down hierarchies with a command-and-control structure, and that we can direct people to move to action without meaningful investment.

We'll address why these assumptions are outdated in later chapters, but if you agree that we aren't putting enough energy into activating our strategies after we create them, the antidote here is pretty obvious: we need to begin to invest in activation, not as an add-on or a "nice to have." Ideally, it should be an integral part of any planning process, either a broad strategy or a targeted initiative within an organization.

As a rule of thumb, if the strategy is outsourced, expect to invest 20 to 30 percent of the cost of strategy development to fund the activation plan itself, and to manage an activation program in a large organization for at least six to twelve months.

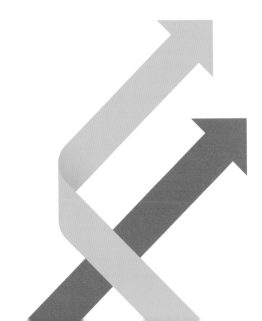

The size and scope of a successful activation program varies widely, of course, based on a series of factors:

- **How large is the organization?** The larger the organization, the more exponential the complexity of growing networks of stakeholders and their unique needs.

- **How entrenched or adaptive is the organizational culture?** More agile, adaptive cultures absorb change more rapidly, often requiring a smaller-scale program over a shorter timeframe than more change-resistant cultures.

- **Is decision-making more hierarchical and top-down or flat and distributed?** The more distributed and autonomous the decision-making power, the greater the investment.

- **How many different stakeholder groups?** More stakeholder groups result in a broader array of unique needs to be addressed.

- **Does the program encompass multiple regions, languages, or cultures?** Strategy shifts require culture change, and programs will need to be tailored for each unique environment.

- **What investment are you willing to make to achieve an accelerated pace of change?** All other factors being equal, an activation plan can be accelerated, but it will take a heavier investment.

Bottom line: We need to include activation planning as an elemental part of strategic planning for any transformative endeavor. If we're not asking how to get our team on board and what we're willing to invest to ensure adoption, alignment, and execution, we're missing the largest opportunity to be part of the 20 percent of strategies that succeed.

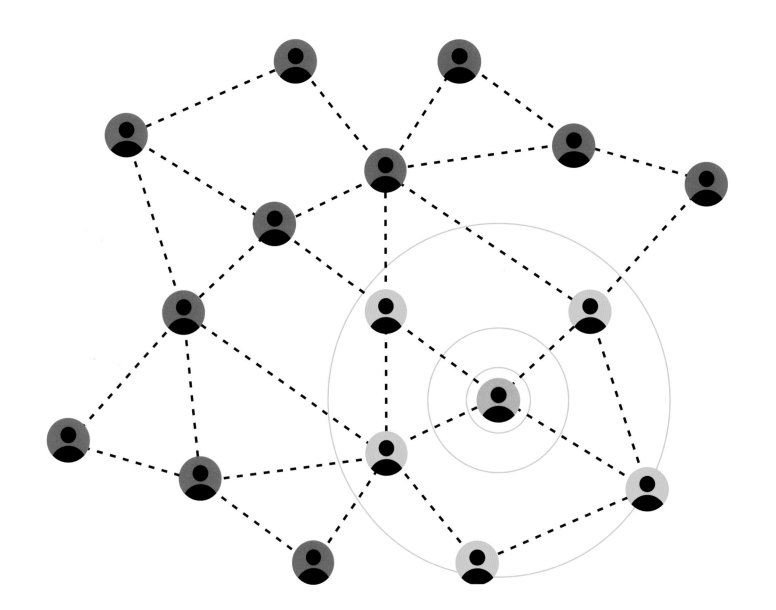

part 2
a new paradigm: from change management to activation

The Organization as a Machine: An Outdated Concept

Our current approach to leading change in organizations didn't happen by accident—it was the product of the era in which most management thinking developed.

We must look to history to understand how we got here. The modern organization is rooted in military history—at the time, the most efficient model for coordinating large groups of people to achieve strategic objectives. Though groups of humans have been collaborating throughout history, warfare hatched the first large-scale mobilization and coordination of resources united in an organizational structure. It has been present as a model for at least 10,000 years.

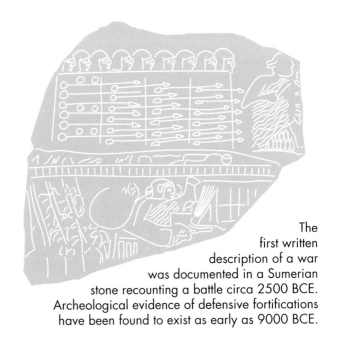

As we entered the Industrial Age, which required large groups of people working in a coordinated way, it was natural to leverage the military model as the most efficient model for corporate organizational structure.

Most managers had risen from the ranks of military experience, further entrenching military discipline and norms throughout the emerging corporate structure. This remained true through the formation of modern business schools, whose coming of age occurred on the heels of World War II.

The first written description of a war was documented in a Sumerian stone recounting a battle circa 2500 BCE. Archeological evidence of defensive fortifications have been found to exist as early as 9000 BCE.

The impact of these influences remains today. It shows up in the language of business, for example—think of all the business jargon that clearly has military roots. Our actions are defined by *missions, strategies,* and *tactics,* which we roll out at *all-hands* meetings. In marketing, *we defend our position* to ensure that we don't *lose ground.* To *capture* market share, we might use *guerilla marketing.* We talk about the *chain of command,* including *leadership ranks* and their *subordinates,* the *boots on the ground,* and their *frontline* managers. We give people *promotions* and *honor their years of service.* Even my own business school was organized into *cohorts*—a structure modeled after the Roman legions.

Historically, men predominantly led and populated armies, lending not only an overtly military language to business but also a masculine one, impacting not only the words of business but also its culture. The structure favored men, creating a highly homogenous workforce, which was hostile to diversity of all types, especially women. These impacts are also still apparent, with 94 percent of current Fortune 500 CEOs being male and 68 percent of those being white.[1]

As a result, we've been trained to think of organizations as homogenous and mechanistic, with a clear set of rules, a command-and-control structure, and the ability to leverage hierarchy to get things done quickly by issuing top-down directives to reallocate resources to meet objectives.

The metaphor of the organization as a machine becomes apparent—an easily programmable structure that will run the "program" that we define, and then pivot in a new direction as soon as we provide new instructions.

By and large, this was true up until the end of the 20th century. The corporate structure and the needs of the organization were tantamount, and the individuals in the system were seen as "human resources"—in effect cogs in the wheels of the machine, easily replaceable when they wore out.

This was easier to maintain with a homogenous workforce, leaders trained in the command-and-control mindset, and a prevailing system stacked in favor of the employer. For most of modern history, this was the context that ruled the world of work.

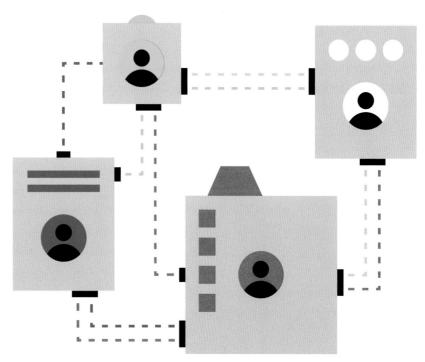

What changed? A number of factors:

The influence of military tradition is on the retreat

The untangling of the military from modern organizations is accelerating, and its influence is waning. When President Dwight Eisenhower described the intersection of military and corporate entities as the military-industrial complex in his farewell address of 1961, military spending represented 9 percent of the U.S. economy. Today, that has shrunk by two-thirds to 3 percent, driven by reduced peacetime spending, technological efficiencies of scale, and privatization.[2]

In addition to the military playing a smaller part in our overall economy, it also employs significantly fewer people and plays a much smaller part in the grooming of our leadership ranks (pardon the military jargon). According to research by Benmelech and Frydman, as recently as 1980, 59 percent of the CEOs of large public corporations had served in the military. By 2013, only 6 percent were led by CEOs with military experience.[3]

As a result, the influence of structure, process, language, and behaviors rooted in the military experience are waning in our organizations, creating space for new ways of being and a proliferation of different models of organizational design and management.

The modern workforce has greater power and increased protections

While labor revolts like the peasant revolts in medieval England have occurred throughout history when workers rose up to fight for fair working conditions, the Industrial Age elevated this to a human rights issue at a scale too large to ignore.

Though power was once universally in the hands of employers, in the last century global labor rights movements have shifted the balance of power towards employees.

This was accelerated by the advent and influence of global organizations. In 1919, the International Labour Organization (ILO) was formed as part of the League of Nations to protect workers' rights, and this organization was later incorporated into the United Nations.

Under the United Nations, several workers' rights were described and incorporated into two articles of the Universal Declaration of Human Rights of 1948, which has now been signed by 192 nations.

While we may take these changes for granted, it is important to understand that it's been less than a century since these rights were acknowledged, let alone implemented.

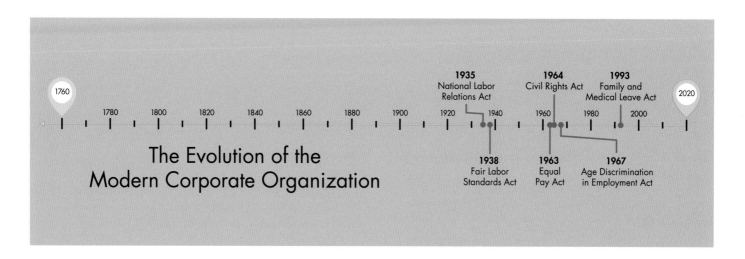

The Evolution of the Modern Corporate Organization

Timeline from 1760 to 2020:
- **1935** National Labor Relations Act
- **1938** Fair Labor Standards Act
- **1964** Civil Rights Act
- **1963** Equal Pay Act
- **1993** Family and Medical Leave Act
- **1967** Age Discrimination in Employment Act

In the United States, for example:

- It wasn't until 1935 that the National Labor Relations Act enshrined labor rights in the nation.

- It wasn't until 1938 that the Fair Labor Standards Act first made accommodations for the establishment of an eight-hour workday, time-and-a-half pay for overtime, and clear limitations around child labor.

- It wasn't until 1963 that the Equal Pay Act sought to abolish wage disparity between genders.

- It wasn't until 1964 that the Civil Rights Act banned discrimination based on race.

- It wasn't until 1967 that the Age Discrimination in Employment Act created protections for older workers.

- It wasn't until 1993 that the Family and Medical Leave Act ensured that workers have job-protected (but unpaid) leave for qualified medical and family reasons.

Let's pause to realize how recent these changes are. If we consider the era of the modern corporate organization to have begun around 1760, at the beginning of the Industrial Revolution, we have only recently seen these significant shifts in the balance of power between employers and employees.

These changes paved the way for the organization to become less of a machine and more like an organism: in balance, with employees empowered as stakeholders in the system. While we have a long way to go, it makes sense that these shifts require us to consider how our old systems of managing change need to change.

The modern workforce is less homogenous

Our workforce is more diverse than it has ever been, and this shift is accelerating as the structures of homogeny are being actively removed.

Women's share of the labor force has undergone a major transformation since 1950. The share of women in the labor force grew from 30 percent in 1950 to almost 47 percent in 2000, and is projected to be above 48 percent by 2050.[4]

Racial diversity is also increasing more rapidly than ever. According to research:[4]

- The share of white non-Hispanics is anticipated to decrease from 73 percent in 2000 to 53 percent in 2050.
- Meanwhile, Hispanics are expected to more than double their share of the labor force, from 11 percent in 2000 to 24 percent in 2050.
- Blacks also are expected to increase their share from 12 percent in 2000 to 14 percent in 2050.
- Asians, the fastest-growing group in the labor force, are projected to increase their share from 5 percent to 11 percent between 2000 and 2050.

This increasing diversity is occurring across many dimensions. Workforces are increasingly comprised of individuals of different genders, religions, races, ages, ethnicities, sexual orientations, educations, and lived experiences, resulting in dramatically less homogenous organizations.

The Big Shift

The above shifts are part of a much bigger change taking place in business. While each and every one of them has contributed to the shift in our current context, there's also a larger story to tell.

Probably most transformational, the very basis of competition has shifted in the modern world: from productivity, efficiency, and output to creativity, innovation, and purpose.

The systems we live and work in were designed in the past. They were created to serve the Industrial Age, which valued productivity, efficiency, and return on capital above all. The systems did the job they were supposed to do, but they didn't anticipate where we were headed: into an age where human creativity is the most valuable resource.

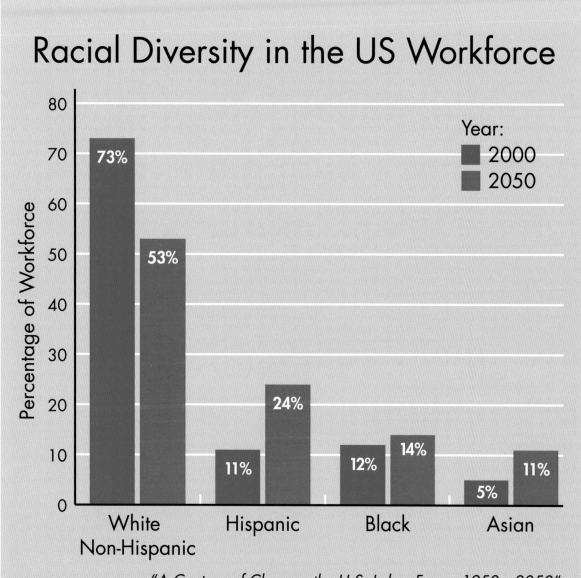

Racial Diversity in the US Workforce

Percentage of Workforce

Year:
■ 2000
■ 2050

- White Non-Hispanic: 73% (2000), 53% (2050)
- Hispanic: 11% (2000), 24% (2050)
- Black: 12% (2000), 14% (2050)
- Asian: 5% (2000), 11% (2050)

"A Century of Change: the U.S. Labor Force, 1950—2050"
US Bureau of Labor Statistics

I am convinced of one thing—that in the future, talent, more than capital, will represent the critical factor of production.

—Klaus Schwab

As Klaus Schwab, executive chairman of the World Economic Forum and author of *The Fourth Industrial Revolution*, states: "I am convinced of one thing—that in the future, talent, more than capital, will represent the critical factor of production."[5]

Schwab and others who are tracking the history of the organization point to why employee engagement and investment in activation to achieve change has become so important.

We can think of the history of the organization as occurring in four broad ages:

1. **The Agrarian Age:** As humans began to grow their own food, they formed cooperative partnerships to distribute labor. The primary basis of competition was strength and stamina, and the organizational structure was small groups of individuals with shared interests.

The Evolving Role of the Organization and Its People

	Agrarian	Industrial	Information	Purpose
Employee Value Proposition	Survival	Satisfaction	Engagement	Meaning and fulfillment
Desired Employee Characteristic	Strength	Efficiency	Knowledge and curiosity	Self-awareness
Development Focus	Stamina	Craft mastery	Creativity and innovation	Purpose

Based on The Fourth Industrial Revolution, Klaus Schwab

2. **The Industrial Age:** In the 18th century, as trade provided access to a diversity of natural resources, technology improved and capital was consolidated to create entities that could increase the value of basic resources. Labor became a commodity in service of capital. The basis of competition was efficiency and overall organizational output, with the organization relying on a subservient labor structure.

3. **The Information Age:** Beginning in the 1970s, it became more profitable to add value to information than to natural resources. While both models coexisted, a shift began in the role humans would play in the organization of the future. The emerging basis of competition was creativity and innovation, requiring a flexible organizational structure and an empowered workforce.

And even though we're only just catching up to that reality, we're already moving into the next age:

4. **The Purpose Age:** As improved quality of life becomes more accessible for more humans and basic needs are met with the help of the technological advancements of the Information Age, organizations shift to serving human wants and needs more effectively. As a result, self-awareness and empathy become more important, with an emerging organizing structure based on self-selection around a common purpose.

As we look at the evolution of business over time, it becomes apparent what's happening: The business models we're operating under are trailing the era in which we live today. Our structures have remained largely remnants of the Industrial Age, even as we've been living in the Information Age. And while we're catching up to that shift, we are yet again already moving into the next age – Purpose.

As leaders, we need to take a longer perspective on what's happening around us to anticipate the direction of change and begin building new approaches today to guiding change in our organizations tomorrow.

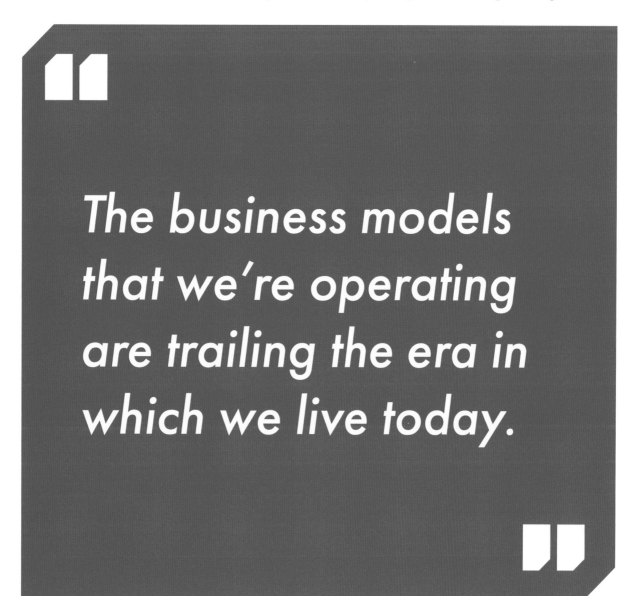

The business models that we're operating are trailing the era in which we live today.

The Living Organization

If the model of the organization as a machine is becoming obsolete, what is emerging to take its place?

To meet the needs of the Information Age, our organizations must nurture increased creativity and innovation, which requires us to encourage empowerment, entrepreneurial thinking, and risk-taking. In order to be competitive, the very structure of the organization must shift to create an environment in which empowered and creative employees will thrive.

As the Purpose Age emerges, we'll also need to support employees' ability to find meaning in their work, align themselves with people and projects of shared interests, and elevate communication and collaboration through increased empathy and co-creation.

This begins to look more and more like independent bodies aligning themselves in constantly changing structures to achieve common outcomes—like atomic particles organizing to form a molecule, or molecules forming an organism. An organism actively and collectively senses changes in its environment and adapts itself and its reactions in response.

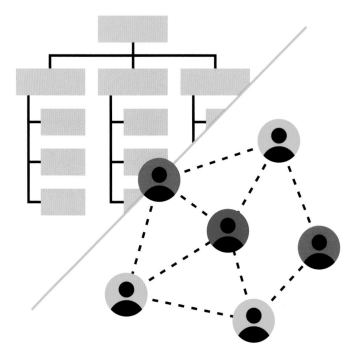

In his book *The Living Organization*, Norman Wolfe posits that organizations are now more like organisms: living, changing beings that adapt to new environments and shift in response:

"Like people, plants, and other living organisms, corporations are born, grow old, and die. They are governed by the same laws of life as other living beings and follow the same hierarchy of need fulfillment as people do. They are an intrinsic part of life, particularly in our post-modern society. They marry through mergers and give rise to offspring (or spin-offs). When they mature, they have the choice of rebirthing, of branching off in new directions (new markets, new products, or totally new business models), or withering away and dying."[6]

This makes intuitive sense—organizations are groups of humans united to achieve a common goal. In fact, the word "corporation" comes from the Latin *corpus*, meaning body.

While all this may be obvious, the implications are immense, so let's look a little deeper at how organizations are more like organisms than machines. Here's Merriam-Webster's definition of an organism:

organism

or·gan·ism | \ ˈȯr-gə-ˌni-zəm \
Definition of *organism*

1: a complex structure of interdependent and subordinate elements whose relations and properties are largely determined by their function in the whole

2: an individual constituted to carry on the activities of life by means of parts or organs more or less separate in function but mutually dependent: a living being

Some alternate definitions:

- A whole with interdependent parts, likened to a living being

- A form of life composed of mutually interdependent parts that maintain various vital processes

- Any complex thing or system having properties and functions determined not only by the properties and relations of its individual parts, but by the character of the whole that they compose and by the relations of the parts to the whole

Beyond definitions, we can look at the traits that define an organism to see if the analogy holds up. If you consult a biology textbook, you'll discover that there are eight generally accepted behaviors of an organism:

Organization and cellular composition: Organisms are made up of individual cells, combined into groups of cells or organs, which perform specialized functions in service of the larger organism.

Genetics and heredity: Organisms pass their traits on to subsequent generations of the organism and its progeny.

Homeostasis: Organisms maintain their internal environment to achieve the balance required to perform their desired functions, even in the face of a changing external environment.

Metabolism: Organisms convert nutrients into energy to do work in a series of processes collectively called metabolism.

Growth: Organisms seek to expand their size and scope.

Response to stimuli: Organisms respond to changes in their environment by altering their actions.

Adaptation: Organisms adapt to changing conditions in the long term through adaptations that provide advantages in survival and growth.

Reproduction: Organisms can reproduce themselves to create new organisms.

The most progressive and simple definition of life comes from NASA, whose working definition is: **"Life is a self-sustaining system capable of Darwinian evolution."**[7] It's simple, because it can be communicated clearly in one sentence, and progressive, in that it anticipates the possibility of new characteristics that we don't yet understand.

Whether we look at the modern organization through the lens of NASA's definition or the behaviors that define an organism, we see that the modern organization is increasingly becoming more organism than machine:

Organization and cellular composition: Organizations are made up of individuals (cells), which in turn combine into groups of teams (organs), which perform specialized functions in service of the larger organization.

Genetics and heredity: Organizations pass on mindsets, behaviors, and ways of working through culture to subsequent generations of the organization and its new ventures and spinoffs.

Homeostasis: Organizations maintain their internal environment to achieve the balance required to perform their functions, even in the face of a changing external environment. This shows up in many forms: cycles of hiring and layoffs, budget growth and reduction, and mergers and acquisitions, to name just a few.

Metabolism: Organizations convert resources, such as people and capital, into energy to do work in a series of processes that can collectively be called metabolism.

Growth: Whether in pursuit of greater market share, increased profits, or positive impacts that serve its mission and purpose, organizations seek to expand their size and scope.

Response to stimuli: Organisms respond to changes in their environment by evaluating the competitive environment, market, and areas of opportunity, and altering their actions accordingly.

Adaptation: Organizations adapt to changing conditions over the long term by selecting adaptations that provide advantages in survival and growth. Adaptation drives product strategy and development, mergers, acquisitions, and spinoffs.

Reproduction: Organizations can reproduce themselves to create new organizations, whether direct copies (like franchising or expansion of an existing model into new markets) or evolutionary descendants (such as new ventures, divisions, or brands).

We can see that there's a strong argument in favor of reconsidering our notion of what an organization really is. Returning to the observation that the root of "corporation" is *corpus*, meaning body, maybe we've known this all along.

The more organizations tend towards increased autonomy, diversity, and empowerment, the more they resemble a living organism, made up of diverse and independent people working together as a collective body, constantly adapting and reorganizing itself in response to dynamic conditions.

The Shifting Role of Change Management

If traditional organizational theory sees organizations as machines, traditional change management sees them in terms of processes and routines that can be reordered systemically.

In the modern organization, change shifts from a process-driven, mechanistic model to a more human-centered approach, appealing to the wants and needs of individuals and following a more flexible set of principles to adapt to circumstances.

As the balance of power has shifted, the mindsets and behaviors of the collective define the organization at least as much, if not more, than the organization defines the behaviors of its people.

If we begin thinking of organizations as organisms, some clear implications emerge, and required shifts become apparent:

- From program to persuade: We can't just push a new program or strategy—we need to generate excitement and create pull around a shared vision.

- From command to engage: When control is distributed, we need to persuade more people to gain alignment. We can no longer drive adoption or force buy-in; we need to authentically engage employees to participate in the change.

- From cascade to co-create: The smartest person in the room is the room. We can't throw ideas over the wall—instead, we need to honor the intelligence among our teams by inviting them to co-create better solutions.

- From processes to principles: Every organism is unique and dynamic, and we need to adopt methods to context by creating guardrails instead of rules.

- From homogeny to diversity: People, like cells in our analogy, are each living beings nested within the whole. Both individual people and teams have their own wants and needs. We need to consider the whole spectrum of stakeholders and address them individually. No more "one size fits all" change programs!

Suddenly, we find that the old ways don't work on the new structures. To accomplish change, we can't just reprogram the machine. We need to persuade and engage empowered, thoughtful humans to move in a new direction, at scale. Therefore, we need to rethink how we organize, manage, and lead them.

To do that, we need to redesign our understanding of change management to create a new model that is better suited to meeting the needs and characteristics of our modern organizations.

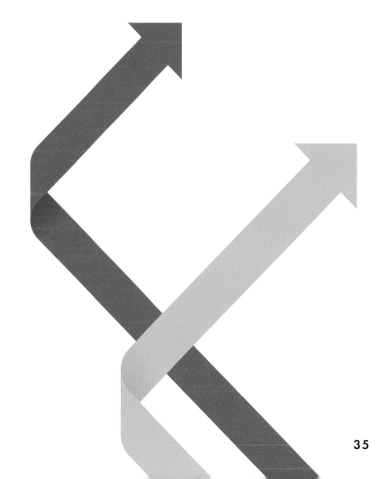

A New Paradigm: From Change Management to Activation

The largest implication of our redefinition (or realization) of the nature of organizations is that the systems we've used in the past to operate and manage organizations also need to evolve, and in some cases be completely replaced.

To activate change, we need to reconsider our approach to change. Just as organizational design was built around the concept of organizations as machines, the field of change management was designed to fit that paradigm, and its mechanisms were designed to work well in a homogenous, hierarchical, command-and-control structure.

Again, language indicates the model that change management was designed for, and we can see this in the words used in its practices. We are told to drive adoption by cascading information, and that we can generate buy-in by building coalitions. These words feel familiar and comfortable in the old model, don't they? But how about now? Even the idea of driving adoption by cascading information assumes a hierarchical structure of people who can be coerced through the ranks.

We also see this to be true in how most change management programs are organized: as a linear process, made up of a series of cumulative, ordered steps, targeted at the level of the organization, not the individual. Whether the change program we utilize has four steps, five steps, seven steps, or eight, they all follow a similar, methodical process that assumes we move the organization along as one. The object is still the organization as a machine, not the individuals in the system.

But do these assumptions apply now? In a world where the organization looks more like an organism and the elemental unit in the system is a mindful, empowered human being, how must our very notion of change management shift?

We don't suggest that change management should be abandoned, but rather that we should upgrade it to meet the needs of the modern organization. If you've been trained in any of the most pervasive change approaches, whether ADKAR, Kotter's Eight Steps, McKinsey's Seven S Framework, or another time-tested approach, keep reading. Each of these models is research-based and field-tested, with great wisdom that still applies. Each can provide a solid framework for the design of an effective program for change.

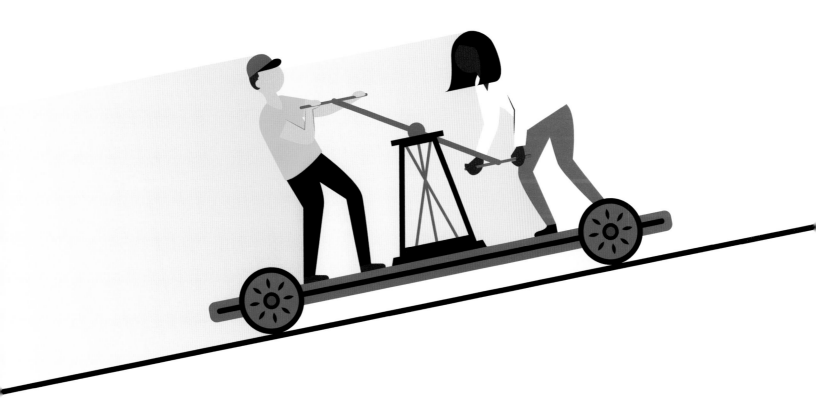

However, we need to evolve our change methodology to meet the emerging needs of the modern organization. That requires looking at the challenge from a human-centered perspective and reconsidering the organization as a vibrant organism. To do that, let's revisit the characteristics of an organism, which we learned earlier:

Organization and cellular composition: If organizations are made up of individuals, which in turn combine into groups of teams to perform specialized functions in service of the larger organization, then we should shape our approach to target individuals, teams, and stakeholder groups rather than treating the organization as a monolith. This is where human-centered design comes in: to design our approach to target the unique wants and needs of the diverse humans and groups of humans in the system.

Genetics and heredity: If organizations pass their mindsets, behaviors, and ways of working, collectively their "culture," on to subsequent generations of the organization and its new ventures and spinoffs, then we need to deeply consider the culture in our work and understand how it works with or against the change we're trying to enact.

Homeostasis: If organizations maintain their internal environment to achieve the balance required to perform their functions, then we need to understand how a change in one area may impact others and anticipate this in our plans.

Metabolism: If organizations convert resources such as people and capital into energy to do work, then we must consider how to properly support people with the resources they need to support the new efforts we require.

Growth: If organizations seek to expand their size and scope according to their purpose, we need to frame the change we seek in terms of how it will advance the organization's larger purpose.

Response to stimuli: If organisms respond to changes in their environment by shifting their actions accordingly, we need to understand and anticipate the external climate and ensure that our changes mitigate or harmonize with external forces.

Adaptation: If organizations adapt to changing conditions over the long term by selecting adaptations that provide advantages in survival and successful continued growth, we should find opportunities to pilot changes and demonstrate success throughout the process so people can experience the positive benefits of the change.

Reproduction: If organizations can reproduce themselves to create new organizations or evolutionary descendants, then we should seek ways to highlight best practices and equip people to replicate them from within.

As we look at organizations as an organism, one thing that stands out above all else is the level at which we need to focus our work: people. Our new model must work at a more elementary level than the monolithic organization— we need to focus on the different wants, needs, and opportunities that exist at levels throughout the organization and adapt our methods accordingly.

We see why even with the best intentions and hefty investments in change programs, we often miss the mark in trying to accelerate change adoption in the modern organization.

We are still designing "one size fits all" change programs, which assume we can move the entire organization forward as one, when in fact we need a more tailored approach that addresses the diverse needs of many individuals.

The better approach, then, is to begin to deeply understand the different needs of various stakeholder groups throughout the organization and to design a program of change that is human-centered. We need to acknowledge that different people and groups of people need different levels of investment and support to reach the same destination.

By investing in deeper levels of understanding and empathy and aligning our approach to known and emergent needs and barriers to change, we stand a much better chance of truly reaching the hearts and minds of the humans within the modern organization—accelerating alignment and realizing our desired results.

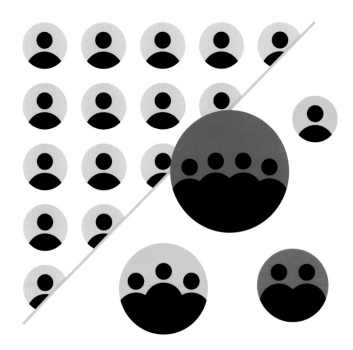

We need to acknowledge that different people and groups of people need different levels of investment and support to reach the same destination.

Strategic Planning - - - - - - - - - - - - - - - -> Strategic Execution

The Activation Abyss

The Rise of Strategy Activation

The term strategy activation began to appear in the 2010s, slowly at first and increasing steadily in popularity in the early 2020s. By 2021, Google appearances of the term were double what they were as recently as 2018–2019. We've seen a corresponding increase in blog posts, webinars, and even consulting practice areas using the term.[8]

There's still a lot of confusion between the terms strategy activation, strategy execution, and strategy implementation.

Many ask, "Aren't they all the same?" Well, no—activation is a step in between. It's the recognition that prior to implementing or executing anything, people must be persuaded to want to make the change. Strategy activation is what comes between the creation of strategy and the execution of strategy.

Most leaders see these as a continuum: "We'll design our strategy, and then it's all about execution!" They try to jump directly from strategic planning to strategy execution. And why not? Don't we just plan the work, then work the plan? Well, yes and no. As an individual or a small team, this may be the case. But with larger organizations, it's not so clear.

In a traditional hierarchical organization, this may be the case. Alignment around the case for change is either implicit or required. Engagement is simpler, because the stakeholder needs are seen as homogenous. Movement to action is seemingly frictionless.

But in our more modern, less hierarchical organization, with its greater diversity, empowerment, and independence of thought, the landscape looks different. The path from planning to execution is not a direct line. In fact, an enormous hidden chasm sits between them. If we don't plan for this—and prepare for how to get our teams across it—we'll never get to the execution side.

So we need to see this gap as the trap that it is. Between strategic planning and execution is a hidden obstacle where strategy goes to die. What most failed change leaders fail to see is something we call the *activation abyss.*

This abyss is ever-present and should be clearly visible, but we are so accustomed to the old ways of command and control that we still assume it's enough just to tell people to cross it.

That doesn't work anymore because employees now have much more agency to decide for themselves if they'll follow you. Remember, you recruited them because they were creative, innovative, even entrepreneurial. You empowered

Strategy Activation is the art and science of persuading people to align around, engage with, and adopt new ways of working in order to achieve a shared vision.

them so they could leverage their intelligence and creativity to accomplish work in new and innovative ways. And—this should go without saying—they think for themselves. You hired critical thinkers who don't just follow orders by design.

Many leaders fail to recognize that between the decision to go to a new place and the actual expedition, a large effort is required to recruit the team, persuade them that your destination is attractive, and support them in preparing for the journey. And it doesn't stop at persuasion: even if you convince them that they want to join you on the trip, you'll need to ensure they are prepared with the skills, knowledge, and equipment to be successful.

We can now see the next piece to this puzzle: How do we bridge the gap between planning and execution, and persuade our teams to join us on the journey?

As change leaders, whether personally leading the transformation or supporting the overall effort, our first job is to make this gap clear for all to see. Recognizing this obstacle and making a plan to cross it safely is the single most important factor in becoming one of the strategies that succeed.

The Investment in Activation

Recall that the lack of investment in activation is one of the main reasons strategies fail. Avoiding this pitfall means investing energy into closing this gap by persuading people to try new ways of working.

Inertia is powerful: it's easiest to do something tomorrow the way I did it yesterday. Before someone is willing to try a new way of doing something, they need to be convinced there's a good reason to do so, and that the new way is better for them than the old way.

To define it clearly, strategy activation is the art and science of persuading people to align around, engage with, and adopt new ways of working in order to achieve a shared vision.

As such, it is a necessary predecessor to implementing or executing a new strategy. It's the connective tissue that helps people see why the change is needed, understand what's required, and be willing to move to action together in a new way.

Only once activation is successful is an organization prepared, equipped, and capable of executing strategy. To implement new ways of working, we need to persuade people to try new things. We need to support them not only with the case for change, but also the learning, training, and support they need to succeed. This process is like training the body for competition, preparing an orchestra for a new performance, or recruiting people to join a social movement. It takes an investment in activation to overcome inertia and move to a new level.

Why has strategy activation become a thing?

Let's go back to the discussion of the changing nature of the organization. When we evolved our mental model from organization as machine to organization as living organism, something happened: at the cellular level, we gave increased agency to the fundamental elements of the system—people. We empowered them to innovate, imagine, and create potential futures, question the current state, and think critically about the why of things. The very basis of competition today is creativity and innovation, and this has required us to develop a system of empowered, independent, critical thinkers.

This is a fundamental shift to the organization. We should not be surprised that it has upended traditional command-and-control structures, along with the flavors of change management which developed in parallel to them.

Hence, we're seeing the rise of a new practice area to accelerate change adoption in organizations: **strategy activation.** It seeks not to drive change into an organization, but rather to work with its people in a human-centered way: to capture their hearts and minds, develop a shared vision, and persuade them to work together to co-create new futures.

This is a seismic shift, and one every leader should understand deeply. As leaders in this changing world, change is our one constant. The ability to navigate it quickly is the new basis for competitive advantage and a requirement for the successful achievement of organizational missions.

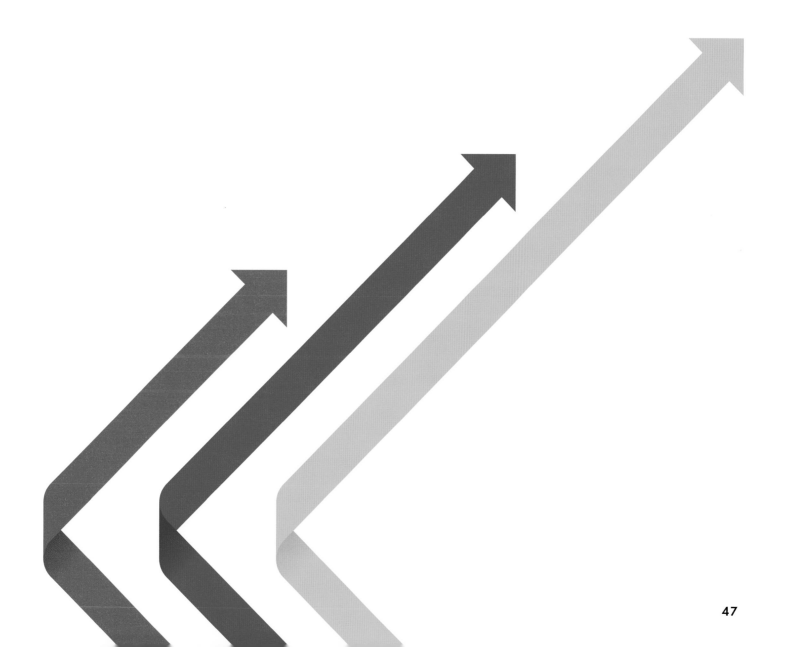

The Business Case for Strategy Activation

If you're persuaded that the old ways don't match our current reality, that organizations now look more like organisms than machines, and that people need activation to move from strategy to execution, you still need to persuade others to make the necessary investment.

For this, let's look for a moment at the business case for strategy activation. While you may see clearly that the need is real, and that success takes investment in activation activities, you still need to build a strong case to secure the necessary resources.

We can frame the business case in terms of expected value: What's the expected value of a transformation effort without a supporting investment in strategy activation versus one that includes such investment? In other words, what is the value of becoming one of the 20 percent of strategies that succeed versus the 80 percent that fail—and how much are we willing to invest to tip the scales?

First let's look at what it costs to ignore it—the most common case today.

To illustrate our point, we'll use a fictional company we'll call Virtucon. Previously a privately-owned and diversified conglomerate, Virtucon has engaged a top-tier management consulting firm to develop a growth strategy to position them for a public offering. They recognize that since the pandemic, they need to shift from an office-based culture to a hybrid workforce, and they need to invest in digital transformation and develop a significantly more robust ecommerce model.

After a $1 million investment in strategy consulting (typical for an engagement like this), the firm has delivered a plan to increase their growth considerably, resulting in a $50 million increase to their top line over the next three to five years. To achieve this, Virtucon will need to shift a major part of their business model and make approximately $10 million of investments in digital automation, new technology, and other costs of execution.

For employees, this will result in major shifts in their ways of working, their roles, and even their reasons for affiliation. They will likely fear how the changes might impact their daily work, perhaps questioning if they fit in this new organization. Many will question why the changes are necessary, whether management understands the implications, and if they will have a job in the new structure. Others will wonder whether they have the skills to meet new challenges and how the company will support them in the transition.

Is this a good investment? Of course, many factors are at play, but we can create a simple model to understand how this might play out by looking at the *expected value* of their investment.

$$EV = \sum P\left(X_i \right) \times X_i$$

Expected value is the anticipated value of an investment at some point in the future, which allows investors to compare options and select the one most likely to maximize their return. It is calculated by multiplying each possible outcome by the likelihood that the outcome will occur and summing those values.

Let's first document our assumptions:

- Cost of the consulting engagement to develop the strategy: $1,000,000

- Expected investments to execute the strategy: $10,000,000

- Financial impact of a successful strategy: $50,000,000

- Percent of strategies that succeed: 20 percent

Using the expected value formula, we multiply the benefit of a successful strategy by its likelihood of achievement, and the cost of the strategy by its likelihood of failure, and add them together. The result looks like this:

Option A: Base Case

$$\left(\begin{array}{c} 20\% \\ \times \\ \$50\ \text{million} \\ \text{gain} \end{array} \right) + \left(\begin{array}{c} 80\% \\ \times \\ \$11\ \text{million} \\ \text{loss} \end{array} \right) = \begin{array}{c} \$1.2 \\ \text{million} \end{array}$$

$1.2 million. That's not a very attractive expected value for an $11 million investment.

Now let's consider some of the hidden costs that aren't captured in these numbers. Fear of change can result in significant loss of productivity. Some employees will wait and see, demotivated to stretch, take risks, and innovate until the dust clears. Others will choose to leave for more secure roles elsewhere. Often those that leave an uncertain environment are the best employees with the most marketable skills, magnifying the impact of turnover and further depleting the return on this investment.

Now let's introduce another factor: the recommendation that organizations invest 20 to 30 percent of the cost of strategy development in activation activities. If we split the difference and recommend that Virtucon spend 25 percent on strategy activation to improve their chances of success, let's see how that impacts the expected value.

Let's say Virtucon decides to invest $250,000 in a strategy activation campaign. First, they develop a clear case for change, outlining the shifting business factors that require the company to do things differently. They paint a clear picture of how they'll be worse off if they don't change.

Next, they develop a clear vision of the better future they envision, with a clear roadmap for how the organization can get there in a series of concrete steps.

Virtucon then supports their employees by developing a series of communications, learning programs, and job aids targeted at specific groups in the company who need tailored support to help them make the transition—building people's confidence and trust and alleviating their concerns.

Finally, they install a series of feedback loops—surveys, focus groups, or other sorts of listening posts—to understand what's working and where people still need support, and respond with targeted help.

With this investment in strategy activation, what happens? Does Virtucon increase their odds of success while mitigating some of the hidden costs? What if the investment raises their chances of success from 20 percent to 50 percent—even odds?

The numbers look like this:

- Cost of the consulting engagement to develop the strategy: $1,000,000

- Expected investments to execute the strategy: $10,000,000

- **Investment in strategy activation: $250,000**

- Financial impact of a successful strategy: $50,000,000

- **Percent of strategies that succeed: 50 percent**

With these assumptions, Virtucon's results look like this:

Option B: Likely Case

$$\left(\begin{array}{c} 50\% \\ \times \\ \$50 \text{ million} \\ \text{gain} \end{array} \right) + \left(\begin{array}{c} 50\% \\ \times \\ \$11.25 \text{ million} \\ \text{loss} \end{array} \right) = \begin{array}{c} \$19.5 \\ \text{million} \end{array}$$

Our hypothetical $250,000 investment in strategy activation yields a 16x increase in the expected value of Virtucon's strategy investment. Given the much larger costs of strategy execution, this seems like a very reasonable insurance policy to tilt the odds in their favor.

In addition, their most critical resource—people—will understand the need for change, be aligned with their vision, and be engaged in supporting it because they feel supported. In addition to increasing Virtucon's chances of success, they also reduce the hidden costs of lower productivity and attrition.

What would it take to raise the odds further to better ensure Virtucon is in the 20 percent of strategies that succeed?

You might say at this point that we shouldn't expect that an investment in strategy activation will guarantee that we'll be part of the 20 percent of companies that succeed, and you're absolutely right. There are many factors at play that we haven't considered, including the quality of the strategy itself, internal capabilities, external forces, and the unforeseen changes that could occur in our broader context, to name a few. This is definitely a very rosy best case scenario we seek to create.

However, the numbers suggest that there continues to be a return on even higher investment in strategy activation. We have no way of calculating the ideal investment, but we do know that there's lots of upside potential, and the investment can scale to generate even better odds of success and higher expected value.

Let's assume that Virtucon decides that their organization is deeply entrenched and resistant to change, and needs a larger investment than $250,000 to address everything needed to gain alignment and move forward as one. They quadruple the budget to $1,000,000, equal to what they spent on the strategy itself.

Is it worth it?

If we change the strategy activation budget to $1,000,000 and as a result assume that the investment increases our chance of success to 80 percent, we get these numbers:

- Cost of the consulting engagement to develop the strategy: $1,000,000

- Expected investments to execute the strategy: $10,000,000

- **Investment in strategy activation: $1,000,000**

- Financial impact of a successful strategy: $50,000,000

- **Percent of strategies that succeed: 80 percent**

With these assumptions, Virtucon's results look like this:

Option C: Best Case

$$\left(\begin{matrix} 80\% \\ \times \\ \$50 \text{ million} \\ \text{gain} \end{matrix} \right) + \left(\begin{matrix} 20\% \\ \times \\ \$12 \text{ million} \\ \text{loss} \end{matrix} \right) = \begin{matrix} \$37.8 \\ \text{million} \end{matrix}$$

Wow—that's an even better picture. More than 30 times better, in fact, than the base case, even with a million-dollar added investment.

I'm not suggesting that your organization needs to invest at this scale. Based on our observations doing this work over the past two decades, I stand by my assertion that an investment of 20 to 30 percent of your strategy development costs can make a material impact on your success. What I am suggesting is that you can't afford not to invest in this important work, and that the return on investment at almost any level is clear.

This assertion is borne out by recent research by London, Madner, and Skerritt at McKinsey and Company.[9] After studying 60 organizations at least two years into major transformations, they discovered a number of things that validate our business case. They found, for instance, that of these companies, the average organization only actively engaged two percent of employees in transformation activities, including the ownership of milestones or engagement in key initiatives. This describes our base case.

They then found, consistent with our better case, that companies that engaged at least seven percent of employees in the transformation were twice as likely as those that didn't to achieve total returns to shareholders (TRS) that exceeded their representative sector and geographic stock index.

And, consistent with our best case, as this effort was scaled even more broadly, the returns grew consistently. With 21 to

30 percent employee involvement, the TRS increased 67 percent over the benchmark.

And critically, those that engaged fewer than this tipping point of 7 percent in fact achieved negative excess TRS—in effect, they lost ground.

The authors stated: "Leaders should think of 7 percent as a bare minimum that is both a catalyst and a guide to secure involvement across all functions and geographies that the transformation will affect. If 7 percent of employees were somehow isolated while the remaining 93 percent continued with business as usual, that wouldn't work. The power of attaining the 7 percent threshold lies in the breadth of reach that it achieves as employees realize that the transformation is not a distant project but rather a fundamental change in how they work. At 7 percent, transformation-initiative owners can no longer be ignored.[9]"

Of course, as any marketing for investment vehicles always states clearly, your results may vary. But the core lesson is clear: the investment in engaging a broad base of employees in strategy activation activities is one of the largest levers you can deploy to increase your chances of success. And in the process, you'll increase employee engagement and alignment, retain your best talent, and accelerate your results.

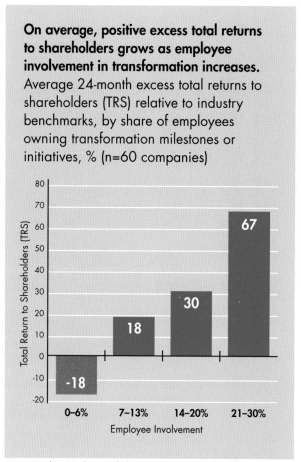

On average, positive excess total returns to shareholders grows as employee involvement in transformation increases. Average 24-month excess total returns to shareholders (TRS) relative to industry benchmarks, by share of employees owning transformation milestones or initiatives, % (n=60 companies)

London, Madner, and Skerritt at McKinsey and Company

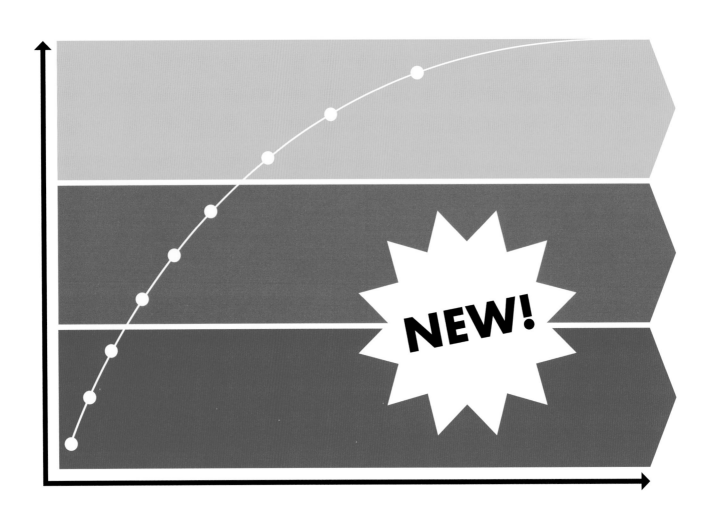

part 3
a new model:
the activation curve

Introduction to the Activation Curve

At this point, it's useful to provide a new framework to better understand what strategy activation looks like in practice.

Because traditional change management grew out of the old model, it is process-centric rather than human-centric, and targeted at the organization as a whole, rather than the unique people within.

The Activation Curve

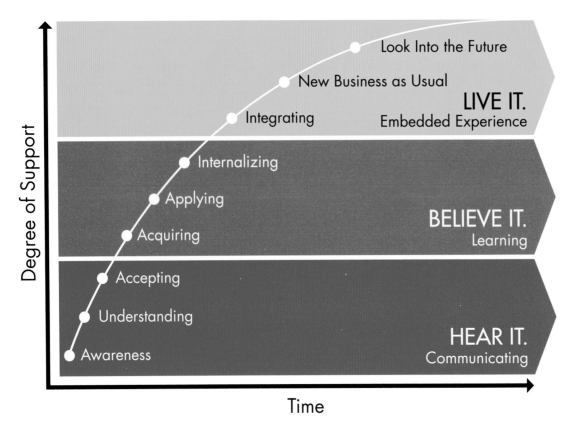

Step 3: Live It
The ongoing behavior change that is necessary to get the changes to stick long-term.

Step 2: Believe It
Creating focused learning tools and experiences to help audiences internalize the changes.

Step 1: Hear It
Communicating the "What" and "Why" behind the change and business need.

This latter point is the most important. As we said earlier, if you are currently using one of the proven change methodologies, you don't need to blow it up or throw it away. The core ideas are sound. Most speak to the need to create a case for change, a clear and compelling vision, a coalition of leaders, and investments in communications and new capabilities.

What needs to change is the focus. Instead of creating a single program focused on moving the organization as a whole, we need to create an approach that's tailored to the unique needs of individuals.

Let's start by upgrading to a framework that is built for the modern organization, designed around people, and describes the journey by which people learn and adapt new ways of working. We call this the activation curve.

The activation curve is the core framework we'll use throughout this book as our model for change. You'll note right away that it's human-centered—written from the perspective of a person inside of a change effort—and that it progresses along a path of learning and development from an individual's point of view.

This is because the activation curve has its roots in learning theory, not change management. It describes how people learn new information, develop new skills and ways of working, and select those that they will utilize in the future.

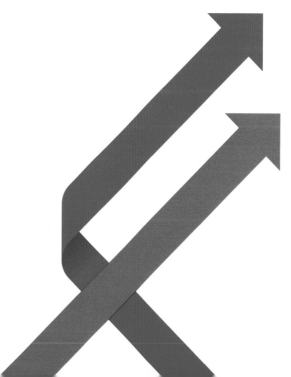

The activation curve describes the journey in terms of three phases:

In the first phase, communication is the primary activity. We seek to have everyone in the organization become *aware* of the proposed change, *understand* the case for change and its implications for them, and (we hope) *accept* that the change is happening and take steps to move forward with it. Importantly, acceptance in this model isn't the same as buy-in, or total agreement. Rather, our goal at this stage is for people to accept the opportunity to try new ways of working, which is the principal transition required to move to the next phase.

To exit the Hear It phase, we seek to have the people open to trying new things. They are still empowered to change their minds, and in the end may not support the change, but they are willing to take the next steps forward to prove it for themselves.

The second phase is all about learning: trying new ways of working and validating that they are better or worse than the old ways. We need to support people with clear roadmaps of what is expected of them, then provide them with learning, skills-building activities, and job aids to support working in new ways.

The first step is to *acquire* the skills or support to try new ways of working, then *apply* those new approaches in the work, which enables people to then *internalize* the results, answering the question for themselves: "Is this better than the way I used to do it?"

Our goal in this phase is to equip people with what's needed to adopt new ways of working and have them internalize and adopt those changes as improvements over the past. Once a majority of our key stakeholders have done this, we enter the Live It phase.

LIVE IT.
Embedded Experience

The goal of the Live It phase is to embed the transformation and make it stick. In essence, we want the change to become the new business as usual.

To achieve this, we need to *integrate* these new ways of working into the DNA of the organization—from onboarding materials to incentive plans and reward systems, process maps to learning and development programs. We need to overhaul our systems, processes, and rituals to ensure that they harmonize with the new way and to eliminate any conflicting remnants of the past that might hold us back.

Culturally, we need to feel that this is now business as usual and have that reflected in the norms and day-to-day behaviors shared by current and incoming employees.

We'll know we've made it when each person feels empowered to begin finding new and even better ways of working. This is the sign that we've achieved our initial objectives and we're ready for new growth.

Stepping back for a moment, let's observe a few things about this model:

- **It's human centered.** This framework is anchored around people, not process. We don't focus our effort on a monolithic organization—we focus on the unique needs of people within it.

- **It describes an individual's learning journey.** Change is all about learning new ways of doing things, which requires an understanding of how people learn and the steps required to support their learning journeys. This is a methodical and cumulative process, but it occurs at an individual level, and the order of activities matters.

- **It respects the reality that people are empowered and will make their own decisions**. The pace of change is determined by the learners. No matter what your process, you won't move the organization from Hear It to Believe It until most people in the system are persuaded that your vision is clear and acknowledge the case for why they should change, resulting in willingness to accept change and experiment with new ways of working. The people are in the driver's seat.

- **It outlines the need for mutual investment.** This isn't a one-way street. It's clear, especially in the Believe It phase, that investments must be made on both sides. While individuals must be willing to try new things, the organization must provide training and tools that equip them to do so.

- **It makes clear that "one size fits all" change management doesn't work.** Not everyone moves through this journey at the same pace, and some need different investments than others to progress. Entire groups within your organization may be hearing it for the first time, while others are already living it. The organization won't achieve its objectives until the majority have moved through each stage. It takes time and differing investments to achieve a broad degree of support.

When we take these factors into account, we can see clearly that top-down, "one size fits all" change approaches are doomed to fail with today's more empowered, diverse workforce, because they assume all people in the organization will move up the activation curve at the same pace.

Keep this framework in mind and refer to it often, as it forms the scaffolding for the topics we're about to explore about how to successfully shape this journey.

People cannot execute a strategy that they don't understand, and they will not execute a strategy that they don't believe in.

—Dave Gray

It's About Creating a Movement

XPLANE founder Dave Gray had a saying: "People cannot execute a strategy that they don't understand, and they will not execute a strategy that they don't believe in."

This highlights an important element of strategy activation: it's not just about understanding, it's about belief. For people to unite and move forward together, they need to believe in the cause—not just intellectually, but in their hearts.

And I'll push this thinking one step further. That belief must be so strong that people are willing to take risks and participate in changing their status quo. Remember that inertia is a powerful force, which must be overcome before change can happen. In the old model, organizations might have overcome this inertia by pushing to a new place. In the new model, people are empowered to make more choices, so we need to create pull to engage people to want to make changes.

In this sense, strategy activation is more like creating a movement: finding a common purpose to align and activate people to change their status quo. Note we didn't say "agree with" or even "buy into" the change. It's not just about gaining agreement that it's a good idea. The focus must be on activating people to change their status quo—a

What is a Movement?
A group of people with a shared purpose who can create change together. It is made up of:

Powerful grassroots support   A shared goal and plan for the future   Solid partner-ships   A strong pipeline of leaders

Inspired by the Global Fund for Women

much higher bar. We need them to actively participate in making the change real.

In numerous studies of social movements across the years, the question of what motivates or demotivates participation has been a central focus. When a group of people share a grievance or a vision for change, why is it that only a small percentage act on it—and what can be learned about how to tip the scales?

A famous study in the 1980s by Bert Klandermans and Dirk Oegema looked at this very question.[1] They studied efforts of the Dutch peace movement to mobilize citizens to protest and act against the deployment of cruise missiles, a very unpopular action. In one study, they found that 75 percent of participants in a random community sample were sympathetic to the goals of the movement, but fewer than 5 percent of those actually participated in a protest or other event to show solidarity and make change. These people not only understood the issue but also believed in the cause, yet fewer than 1 in 20 people took action.

The researchers discovered that three primary factors contributed to this low rate of participation:

1. Sixty percent of those sympathetic to the cause reported that they weren't targeted or recruited to participate.

2. Of those who were targeted, only 17 percent said they had sufficient motivation to participate.

3. Of those who intended to participate, only 33 percent actually showed up. (Life happens!)

If we were to create a rough model to see what this study suggests about strategy activation, it might look like this:

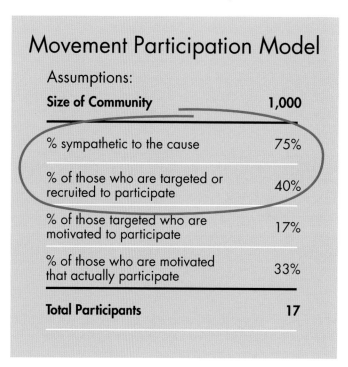

Movement Participation Model

Assumptions:

Size of Community	**1,000**
% sympathetic to the cause	75%
% of those who are targeted or recruited to participate	40%
% of those targeted who are motivated to participate	17%
% of those who are motivated that actually participate	33%
Total Participants	**17**

If our employee population was 1,000 people, and we needed to activate a larger percentage to join our cause in order to succeed in gaining momentum for change, you can see where we need to make the most effort.

First, we need to ensure that we win the hearts and minds of a majority of people and persuade them to join those sympathetic to our cause. This is where our clear vision and case for change come in. We absolutely must achieve a significant majority here, or the numbers just won't work.

Second, once we have a significant sympathetic population, we need to take a further step and actively engage them. It's not enough to have them agree with our vision, we need to recruit them to our cause. This is where we build on our vision and add depth by actively engaging employees in strategy activation activities like communications events, learning programs, workshops, and focus groups. Those touchpoints target their participation and recruit them to the cause.

There's one more factor to add to this formula for creating a movement: persistence. We can't just launch the program with a big splash and then move on. We need to develop a consistent cadence of employee engagement activities to build and keep momentum.

Studying religious movements, which are considered fairly "sticky" in their ability to maintain affiliation, researchers Fred Bird and Bill Reimer[2] observed that over 75 percent of those they interviewed in a prior study had dropped out when interviewed two years later. They concluded that typical participants were "transitory affiliates" to movements, people who were involved for a while but dropped out eventually.

These transitory affiliates pose an additional threat to strategy activation programs. If we don't keep this group in mind, we may invest a great effort to develop sympathy for our cause and to recruit and engage employees to join our movement, only to lose them over time to the next big thing (or simply the pressures of their day job). It takes an investment in steady persistence—a targeted cadence of activities over time—to maintain and build the momentum we require.

Our study of social movements offers three important lessons for our activation program:

1. We need to persuade a large majority of our community to become sympathetic to our cause, which requires broad and compelling communications early on.

2. We need to mindfully invite and recruit our community to join our movement and actively engage them in activation activities.

3. We need to be persistent in engaging our community over time to ensure we maintain momentum.

Our program will be more successful if we can persuade people with a clear vision and a case for change, actively invite and recruit a broad base of our community to engage in the change activities, and persist in meeting the needs of our stakeholder groups with a consistent cadence of engagement activities until the goal is accomplished.

Remember the McKinsey research and its 7 percent tipping point? To get past that tipping point, we need to create a movement.

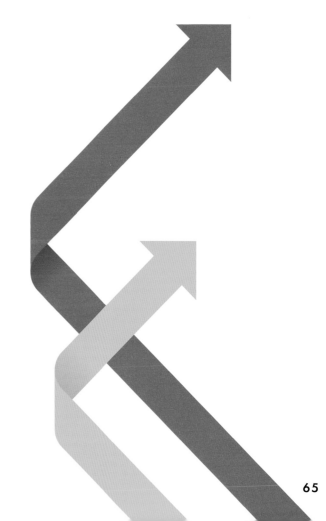

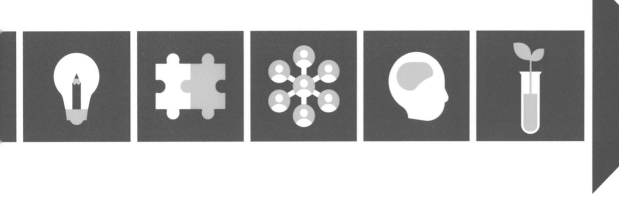

part 4
what strategy activation requires

I remember on one of my first days in business school meeting Jack Gabarro, our instructor for the first-year class on leadership and organizational behavior. Like the sage advisor and storied executive that he is, he opened the day with this prediction: "In twenty years, when I ask you what was the most critical factor in your success, you won't speak of your finance, marketing, operations management, or strategy expertise, you'll tell me about the 'soft stuff' you learned along the way—leadership, communications, employee development—the things that actually move an organization forward."

At the time, like a lot of new prospective MBAs, I was skeptical. I was there to learn the deep secrets of the mechanisms of business, which would equip me to differentiate myself from my peers through superior business acumen. The "soft stuff" wasn't why I came to B-school.

It turns out Jack was right, and his prediction was even more prescient through the lens of how organizations are evolving. Leaders today need to navigate leadership in completely new ways, manage more complex and diverse organizations, invest more effort in inspiring and leading people, and lead change from the front as a core capability.

As leaders, we need to build new skills to lead a modern strategy activation effort. Leaders must develop a much more diverse, multi-disciplinary toolset beyond the lessons of traditional business administration. Classical leadership and management training is still rooted in past models, and even the most progressive business schools are still anchored in models that reflect past ways of working in most of the overall curriculum.

For the new skills, we need to look to new disciplines: those rooted in understanding human behavior and motivation, including disciplines like psychology, sociology, and anthropology, and applied disciplines like design thinking and visual thinking.

From each of these, we'll gather core elements of what we need:

Biology is the study of living organisms and their physiology, behavior, and unique qualities as individuals and groups. From biology, we begin to understand the elemental workings of individuals in the system, and how the system as a whole remains healthy and balanced.

Anchoring ourselves in the metaphor of organizations as organisms, we can better understand how organizations behave—how they seek homeostasis, respond to stimuli and stress, and adapt to change. We also begin to understand the power of culture, which we can think of as an organization's genes—the mindsets and behaviors passed down throughout the organization.

Psychology is the scientific study of the mind and behavior. From psychology, we begin to understand the motivations of individuals, and how to address their unique wants and needs in order for them to engage in adopting new ways of being.

The tools of psychology give us mechanisms to map the minds—individual and collective—of an organization to understand the wants, needs, and motivations of the individuals within. With this understanding, we can begin to clarify the behavior shifts needed to pursue a new vision and identify the potential barriers to change, along with possible antidotes.

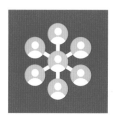

Anthropology is the study of human societies and cultures and their development, interaction, and evolution. Through the lens of anthropology, we see the individual within the network of the system, enabling us to observe the cultures, norms, and behaviors of the group.

We can borrow techniques from anthropology to use empathy and observation to gain a more detailed and nuanced view of the culture of an organization, and the norms and rituals that make it unique. We'll also begin to understand the relative strength of these bonds, and the inertia we'll encounter as we seek to accelerate change.

Design thinking is a process for creative problem solving. Its unique strength is rooted in its human-centered core and its focus on solving the problem at hand from the point of view of the people impacted by the change.

Design thinking injects a new toolkit into problem-solving and solution creation. It leverages empathy (borrowed from anthropology) and utilizes prototyping and iterative design. Ultimately, it shapes the template of co-creation used throughout the activation process to engage employees in the solution development and realization.

For our activation work, we borrow the overall structure and approach from design thinking, anchoring our process to human-centered and iterative design, resulting in both a better solution and a more agile, adaptive one. The iterative design approach also contributes new norms that create space for launching and learning, favoring a bias for action over the traditional bias for perfection.

Design Thinking Process

Empathize	Define	Ideate	Prototype	Test
• Interviews	• Personas	• Share ideas	• Mockups	• Understand impediments
• Shadowing	• Role objectives	• All ideas are worthy	• Storyboards	• What works?
• Seek to understand	• Decisions	• Diverge / converge	• Keep it simple	• Role play
• Non-judgmental	• Challenges	• "Yes and …" thinking	• Fail fast	• Iterate quickly
	• Pain points	• Prioritization	• Iterate quickly	

Stanford d.school

Visual thinking allows people to externalize their internal thinking processes, making them more explicit and actionable. It can also be a way to clarify and organize thoughts, then communicate them visually so groups of people understand new ideas more rapidly and clearly.

The power of visual thinking lies in how humans consume and learn new information. While we often reduce communication to the written and spoken word, in reality language—especially written language—is a new technology for us.

Noah Parsons, a former colleague and expert in data visualization and user experience, points out: "Humans have been communicating with each other for approximately 30,000 years, but we've only been using the written word for about 3,700 years. That's barely 10 percent of the total time that we've been communicating with each other. Because of this long, long history of communicating without text, our brains are simply hard-wired to process visual information better and faster than we process text."[1]

We've been using a combination of information sources, especially visual ones, for much longer than the written word has existed, and our brains are hardwired to consume complex visual information quickly. According to Professor Mriganka Sur of MIT's Department of Brain and Cognitive Sciences, "Half of the human brain is directly or indirectly devoted to processing visual information."[2] Another team of neuroscientists from MIT has found that the human brain can process and recognize images that the eye sees for as little as 13 milliseconds.[3]

As a result, we take in and process visual information more quickly than written or spoken words. Parsons continues: "Part of what helps us process visual information so well is that we can process multiple images simultaneously. With text, we just process one word at a time. When you think about it, that's a pretty slow and inefficient process."

Importantly for our purposes in applying visual information to change programs, visual information is more deeply embedded in the mind, and we retain it longer. According to visual learning expert Dr. Lynell Burmark, "Probably the most compelling reason for using images in instruction is that images are stored in long-term memory. Unlike factoids and phone numbers that can 'go in one ear and out the other,' images are indelibly etched in our long-term memory."[4]

We consider visual communication a core element of the activation toolkit and wherever possible combine words and images to help accelerate understanding. Stanford University's Robert E. Horn explained this relationship clearly: "When words and visual elements are closely entwined, we create something new and we augment our communal intelligence ... visual language has the potential for increasing 'human bandwidth'—the capacity to take in, comprehend, and more efficiently synthesize large amounts of new information."[5]

We'll add visual thinking into our toolkit to inject a turbo-charged approach to visioning and storytelling, which accelerates understanding and alignment. Being able to clearly visualize both the goals and the narrative of an activation program accelerates understanding and adoption.

Your Next Steps in the Journey

Surveying the breadth of these disciplines and their application to being more successful at the "soft stuff," you can see why current MBA programs aren't fully preparing us for leading strategy activation—these disciplines aren't their areas of focus. While leading change is clearly a core capability for the modern leader, formal business curricula have not yet caught up to the more interdisciplinary workings of the modern organization. While many are working towards integrating this kind of thinking—witness the rise of the design MBA (dMBA)—it will take a generation for this to be part of our formal training as leaders.

So your challenge is to do the work and self-study to augment your existing toolkit with some upgrades to enhance your current skills and chosen change management approach in order to lead successful change programs.

The remainder of this book is intended to serve as a toolkit for this journey. It includes basic elements you'll need to combine with specific tools, exercises, principles, and processes to help accelerate change for your organization.

We'll use a journey as the metaphor for our change program, since that's very much what we're trying to achieve: we are asking our organization to take a journey with us to a new place. To do that, we need to clarify the destination, make the case for why it's a desirable place to go, and understand the terrain ahead—including potential obstacles en route, as well as capabilities and constraints. We need a clear plan to get there, and each person needs to know the role they will play in our journey. And we'll need to build in the agility to shift and change our approach as we encounter unforeseen challenges.

There are six key ingredients of a successful activation journey:

Clarity of vision

Do we have a clear vision of our destination that feels motivating and authentic to our organization?

Anticipation of system impacts

Have we anticipated how changes in one part of our structure or organization will impact others?

Stakeholder empathy and understanding

Have we mapped the key stakeholders that will be engaged or impacted by this change, and do we understand their wants and needs?

Alignment of the navigation system

Have we ensured that there is harmony between our mission, values, vision, and strategy?

Awareness of cultural and structural barriers to change

Have we inventoried possible obstacles to change in our culture and context?

Agility to sense, respond, and adapt

Have we designed a system that is flexible and responsive to the inevitable course corrections that will be necessary to succeed?

We'll look at each of these in depth in the following chapters.

Clarity of Vision

When you are planning a journey, especially with others, you likely begin with a destination in mind. You chart a possible course, and you persuade others to join you. Often, it's the destination itself the entices your party to come along. People need to share the desire to reach that destination to join your expedition in the first place.

And yet, remarkably, organizations fail time and time again to make this simple investment. The most overlooked area of opportunity in change work is establishing a clear vision as the first step. Most organizations put the focus on the strategy itself, without making clear that the strategy is a plan to get to a new place (the vision). Many other organizations confuse outcomes with vision: setting a stock price, EBITDA goal, or growth rate as the "vision" for the organization.

I saw this firsthand when I was a young manager working in Silicon Valley in a well-known software company. It was a well-managed organization led by a CEO groomed at General Electric, a fantastic proving ground. At the time, leaders with GE pedigrees were highly sought after due to their rigor and leadership aptitude, and the CEO was and is widely respected.

However, from the inside, the message that was received was that growth and financial success—outcomes—were the "vision" for the coming years. The CEO would consistently and repeatedly—in meetings, town halls, presentations, and posters in the break room—espouse his vision for the company. "Steve's Dream," as it was called, outlined the company's potential stock price and market capitalization as the primary destination for us all to focus on, and the mechanism to achieve high performance. From an employee's perspective, our vision was shareholder success.

This wasn't a vision anchored in meaning or purpose for me as a person. These were financial goals, desired outcomes, metrics and measurements. The message to the team didn't appeal to how we were going to improve the experience of our customers or employees, develop new innovations, or make an impact in the world. It wasn't motivating.

The results? In the three years I worked there, the stock price increased by about two dollars.

So what was missing? This dream didn't speak to the people inside the organization by presenting a clear vision of a better place, a case for changing the path we were on, or how this new approach would help us fulfill our mission or purpose. In fact, this "dream" didn't even describe what we needed to do as a group to achieve the goal. It gave the humans in the system nothing they needed: no clarity on where we were headed, how we would get there, or why we would want to go there in the first place.

The most important single ingredient in activating any new strategy—whether a bold new direction for the overall organization, or a new way of working for a single team—is a *clear and authentic vision that will speak to the hearts and minds of the people responsible and show them the path to realize it.*

Let's break that down into three basic parts:

1. **A clear and authentic vision of the future.** To make it clear, make it visual, make it simple, and make it a story. And it needs to be authentic to be believable and motivating. Authenticity results from anchoring it in the culture and purpose of the organization—does it align with our values, norms, and goals?

2. **The current state and the case for change.** To speak to the hearts and minds of the people responsible, we need to paint a picture of why our current path isn't the right one for the future.

    First, define the current state in a recognizable way. What is our sense of the current state today, and are we in agreement about that? Can we align on what's working, what's not working, and what could be better?

    Next, make the case for change. Is something wrong with the current state? What is the internal or external threat if we stay the same? Organizations, like the people within them, are prone to inertia. What is the reason to move and do things differently?

3. **The roadmap.** To help people see a new path that feels possible and lets them see how they can contribute, show them the big picture. What is the journey from here (current state) to there (future state)? What are the steps on the journey? How do we paint a clear picture of the overall journey and give people a sense that we have a plan for a clear, achievable, and believable course?

We then need to help people understand where they fit and how they contribute. Can they see their specific role, how it contributes to the journey, and their part in the big picture? In addition to the part they play, can they identify with the bigger mission?

> *The more minutely you describe, the more you will confuse the mind of the reader and the more you will remove him from knowledge of the thing described. Therefore it is necessary to make a drawing ... as well as to describe ...*
>
> —Leonardo da Vinci

Before beginning any activation program, you need to develop a clear vision for where you are going, why you are going there, and the route you plan to take. If you can't boil this down to one page, it's not clear enough. We've all seen a 150-page PowerPoint presentation thrown over the wall by the consulting firm, and our skepticism is warranted. This approach is flawed for two reasons:

- People need to understand the big picture before they can progress to deeper levels of understanding.

- People need to believe there's a reason to change before they are willing to invest in change.

Boiling this down to one page is the antidote to both these problems. You need to communicate your vision in one page to enable the elemental unit of change—a person—to see clearly what you see.

The plan also needs to be simple and clear enough to be articulated in one page, ensuring each person can see the role they play in the big picture, and that the picture is complete.

Boiling a vision and strategy down to one page is hard work. Though often attributed to Mark Twain, it was the French philosopher and mathematician Blaise Pascal who first wrote in 1657: "I would have written a shorter letter, but I did not have the time."[6] Creating a one-page roadmap is

worth the effort: it enables you to accelerate understanding and alignment by explaining to others more effectively.

A tool for this is the Vision Map Worksheet: a simple exercise you can use to shape your own thinking or use with others to co-create or articulate a shared vision.

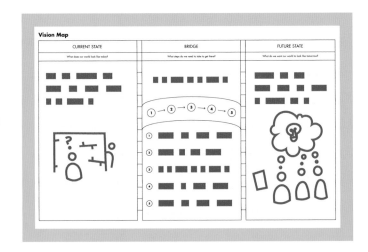

In one page, it combines each of the three key elements discussed earlier: the future vision, the current state and case for change, and the roadmap to get there.

There are many ways to do this, but finding an approach that works for you is foundational to effective strategy activation. You'll need to keep this picture in your mind and its corresponding narrative in your words. Include the vision map in communications to stakeholders to help them see what you see and begin the journey.

Stakeholder Understanding and Empathy

To continue the metaphor of planning a journey, we need to understand who we are inviting to join our expedition, along with their unique wants, needs, and capabilities.

One of the largest implications of our new theory of change—that organizations are organisms made up of people—is that we can't treat them as monoliths. One size does not fit all, and a change management program aimed at the entire organization will likely fail.

For this reason, delivering a single pitch to the entire organization will likely fall flat. By speaking to everyone, we are likely to connect to no one. Tailoring the pitch motivates individuals by speaking to their context and concerns.

Remember that most change management assumes that the top-down hierarchical structure and command-and-control model of traditional business is the status quo. In that environment, it was possible to change an organization's direction through a directive sent from the top.

But we know that's no longer the reality. The truth is that there are as many unique points of view and perspectives on your change as there are people in the organization. Each person has their own wants, needs, fears, and goals, and each will need to evaluate the vision and case for change through their own lens.

We also need each of those people, or at least most of them, to support the change we wish to create. If they don't, and they are working in an empowered environment where control is distributed, our mission will fail.

So we need to understand these perspectives and develop a deep understanding of their context and motivations. This requires empathy—we need to be able to put ourselves in their shoes and see the world through their eyes. Only then can we understand what it will take to successfully persuade them to join us on this journey.

This is where we will draw from the toolkit of design thinking, specifically human-centered design. Empathy is a core tenet of both, the fountainhead from which we turn insights into action.

As a change leader, one of the first muscles you will need to build is your empathy research skill. We will introduce a few ways to use empathy to gather insights, including the empathy map, journey mapping, and user observation and research methods.

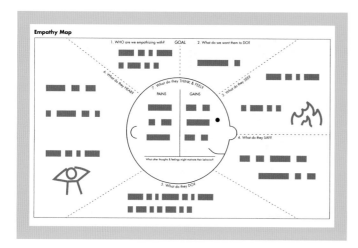

Using the various empathy tools at our disposal, we invest in a deep understanding of the people in our organization, identify common themes for and against the change we seek, and begin to look for commonalities and groupings.

But how can we design a change activation program that addresses the needs of every individual in the organization? Well, of course that's not practical, so we seek to identify a set of stakeholder groups that share similar traits.

We will find groups of stakeholders with similar themes. For example, the product team may be very excited about

a shift to more customer-engaged design, while the sales team is threatened by a change that requires them to give up control of the customer relationship. These two groups have differing wants and needs, and each should be treated differently. The communications, training, and support provided to each group should differ, tailored to our understanding of that stakeholder group.

Once we've developed a deep understanding of the people impacted by the change and mapped their common themes, we'll likely see a clear set of stakeholder groups with common needs.

There's no magic number here, but its typically five to seven different groups in a large organization. That range allows us to speak to the needs of most people in a targeted way, while allowing our program to be scalable with our given time and resources.

Lastly, we want to understand where each group is on a spectrum of support for the change—which are most in support, and which groups are most resistant. Knowing this informs how much investment to make in each group. One group that's already on board may require very little to advance and embrace the change, while another might require a much heavier investment to persuade them to move forward together.

Awareness of Cultural and Structural Barriers to Change

Before embarking on any journey, we'd like to have a map of the terrain ahead. What obstacles will we need to navigate around? What shortcuts might we be able to take? Where do we lack information that we might want to get before we depart?

Drawing again from our design toolkit, this is where the change leader needs to become a bit of an organizational anthropologist and do some deep study to understand its workings.

The question we want to answer is: "What are the barriers to change for this group?" Barriers to change—the obstacles we want to map—are any cultural elements or structural limitations that may slow us down or keep us from reaching our destination. They fall into a few common categories:

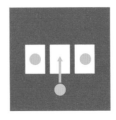

Problem Alignment

Does the organization share an understanding of the problem we're trying to solve and agree it's a problem in the first place?

If no one understands why we need to change, there is no incentive for humans to do anything differently than the way they have been doing it.

We need to develop a clear case for change from the very beginning, conveying both the broad case for organizational change and the narrow case of what this means for individuals.

For example, we worked with a medical equipment company that was losing market share. Even though their sales team was hitting their numbers, competitors were pulling ahead in their ability to attract and retain customers. With some market analysis, the issue was clear: while the company continued to operate a largely transactional approach to selling medical equipment, their competitor was pursuing a more consultative selling approach, uncovering their customers' broad needs, then providing solutions that met these larger needs both for the lab and the hospital system. As a result, they were selling much larger deals while developing longer-term, more strategic relationships. The writing was on the wall.

That said, from the sales team's perspective, the writing wasn't so clear—they were making their quotas, and they didn't have the market-level view to see the larger trend and implications. Absent a clear case for change—how what was happening outside of their view would threaten both the company and their own jobs—they had little incentive to adopt new ways of working and invest in required skill-building.

Until we can answer the question "Why should we change, and how is this better for me?" we won't have problem alignment.

Solution Alignment

Does the organization agree that the solution to the problem is contained in the future state and the roadmap to get there?

Sometimes there's agreement on the case for change, but not on the proposed solution or change approach. This can happen for many reasons, but often it denotes a lack of stakeholder engagement in the process of developing a solution.

For example, we worked with a professional services firm on a customer-centricity initiative, which was initially leader-led. The customer-facing project teams generally agreed with the direction, but not the specific action plans for how to get there. By creating a few pilot teams and sending them to work with customers to refine the proposed approach, they returned with not only a better solution, but a new-found enthusiasm to embrace the work because they saw the impact firsthand.

To develop solution alignment, engage key stakeholders in the process of developing, or at least defining, the solutions to benefit from their insights and give them a sense of ownership.

Fear of the Unknown

What fears might prevent the organization or individuals within it from moving forward?

Fear of the unknown requires that we help people answer the question "What does this mean for me?" through early and frequent communications to mitigate concerns and provide a clear path forward.

Anxiety is a natural outcome of change, as change requires people to move beyond their comfort zone and into unknown territory. In the workplace, this is even more evident, as the security of employees and their families depends on job stability.

For example, we worked on a merger integration project in a software firm. Naturally, the people in the organization that was acquired were fearful of their fate. In truth, the company was acquired because its strengths were highly complementary to the acquiring firm, and the acquirer had every intention to retain and support those teams. They moved very quickly to communicate their intentions to retain staff, showed them a clear path towards integration, and outlined how they would support their career development. They acted quickly to remove fear as an obstacle to integration, retaining top talent that might otherwise have fled in the uncertainty of the transition.

Cultural Barriers

What cultural traditions, rituals, or ways of working present obstacles to our path forward?

Often, change in an organization can run counter to established traditions or common ways of working, resulting in the culture itself being an obstacle to adoption. For example, in our work to help organizations be more customer-centric, a key element is the empowerment of employees at all levels to engage customers in open explorations of their ideas, feedback, and suggestions.

However, if the historical approach to customer interactions has been to present answers first and seek to be the smartest person in the room, the kind of vulnerability and curiosity that good customer-centricity requires runs in direct conflict with established norms. I ran into this conflict head-first as a young consultant. After an attempt to co-create a possible solution with a client, my manager scolded me for asking the client his opinion rather than leading with a recommendation. The old ways were in direct conflict with the new approach, and a culture clash ensued.

To combat cultural barriers to change, we need to make explicit the behavior changes we expect to see, explain the why behind the change, and make it safe to try new ways of working. Tactics include changing people's incentives, public recognition, shared success stories, and role-modeling of new behaviors by leaders.

Interpersonal Barriers

What skills, capabilities, or knowledge gaps will challenge individuals in our organization?

Let's say that the people in the organization see the problem, they agree with the proposed solution, and the solution is in line with cultural values and norms. Smooth sailing, right? Not always—even with these barriers removed, change often requires an investment in building new capabilities, without which people are reluctant to move forward.

For example, we worked with a client that was implementing a new diversity, equity, and inclusion (DEI) program to ensure that equity was woven throughout its core processes and organizational interactions. The employees were very aligned that equity and inclusion was a problem in their community, and that they as an institution could provide clear solutions in their sphere of influence and beyond. Equity was also a core goal of the organization's vision and values, and was woven throughout the strategic plan.

In this case, the barriers were interpersonal ones. The predominantly white organization was aligned with the problem and solution and had cultural alignment as well, but many individuals didn't feel they had the skills or the tools to do the work confidently, respectfully, and successfully.

Interpersonal obstacles can be removed through clear acknowledgment of the issue and commitment to invest in helping employees build the skills and capabilities for new ways of working.

Organizational Capabilities

What organizational capabilities may be lacking that will slow or prevent our progress?

Beyond the individual level, there are often broad organizational capabilities that are necessary to support a transformative change, and if they are lacking, the change will be threatened or at least slowed.

For example, a client wished to strengthen its employee experience and engagement but had no systemic way to gather employee feedback. While it sporadically gathered feedback through manager-led discussions and informal processes, there was no way for employees to provide constructive feedback anonymously, nor to gather feedback broadly and consistently. This gap in organizational capabilities was a clear barrier to executing their program, requiring an investment in survey technology as a first step.

Organizational capability gaps can take many forms, from technology to training, but they share a foundational nature that must be put in place for the organization to move forward.

There are other types of barriers to change beyond these, of course, but you get the idea: if we can surface potential barriers to change before embarking on the journey, we can prepare for them in advance.

Anticipation of barriers informs our work before and all along the journey by helping us to anticipate and mitigate obstacles before they divert us from the path.

Anticipation of System Impacts

When we are planning our journey, we will also need to understand potential impacts of each decision. To go faster in this section of the roadmap, how much more fuel will we need? If we want to send out a scouting party, will we need to backfill the core team to make up for those going ahead? If we want to build a base camp, what additional resources will we require?

Another area that traditional change management overlooks is the unknown impacts or side effects of our actions. Making a change in one area is very likely to cause an impact in another.

Let's return to our analogy of the organization as an organism. We know from biology that an organism seeks homeostasis—balance—and when we impact one part of an organism, its system seeks to rebalance itself. If not, it will get sick or otherwise suffer lessened performance.

The same is true of an organization. If we make a change in one part of the organization—for example, launching a new digital offering—we'll need to make changes in other parts as well, such as marketing, hiring, incentives, and ways of working.

It's important to look at our planned journey and anticipate potential impacts that may occur because of the changes we plan to make, for these are the unforeseen obstacles on our path.

Just as surely as known barriers to change can slow our progress or throw us off course, so too can these unforeseen obstacles. It's best to prepare now and build a response into the plan.

One tool we use to better understand unforeseen impacts is the eight dimensions of an organization:

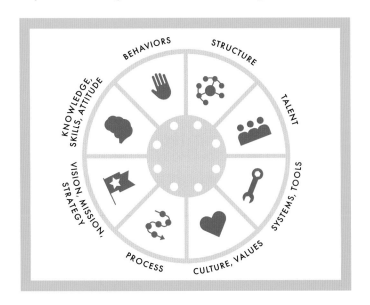

The eight dimensions are core areas of an organization's structure that intersect and collectively shape its success:

- **Vision, Mission, Strategy:** What navigation system guides the organization?

- **Knowledge, Skills, Attitude:** What collective capabilities and mindsets exist in the organization today?

- **Behaviors:** What behaviors define the culture and how it interacts with its stakeholders?

- **Structure:** What is the organizational design of the group?

- **Talent:** What roles and experience exist in the workforce?

- **Systems & Tools:** What tools, technology, and other supporting infrastructure exist to aid the workforce?

- **Culture & Values:** What defines the belief system, rituals, and norms of the people in the organization?

- **Process**: What are accepted processes and ways of working?

A transformation effort may set out to change one or more of these dimensions without considering how the others might be impacted. For example, if we decide to implement a new customer relationship management (CRM) system (Systems & Tools), we're not likely to succeed if we don't also shift our processes and behaviors. When we make a major shift in our vision or strategy, almost all of these dimensions could be impacted.

This type of assessment can reveal powerful insights to inform and improve an activation program:

Required changes to the plan itself. What did we miss? Did a shift in one area highlight a need in another that we'll need to address from the start to succeed? This is a signal that we should take the new information into account and revise our plan to ensure we systematize the linkages and ensure harmony from the start.

Information to share in our communications. How does what we learned inform the content of our communications? How do we get ahead of the issue and address concerns about solutions right from the start? In areas that are "known unknowns," how do we acknowledge that and develop plans to fill in the gaps, or learn as we go so as to relieve the tension of not knowing?

Skills to develop in our training. Change requires new capabilities. What did we learn about where the organization might need support in building new skills, capabilities, or ways of working? How do we design that into our plan to ensure those resources are available when needed?

Anticipating these system impacts early not only results in a better and more realistic plan now, but it also prevents more costly delays that could derail your effort later.

Alignment of the Navigation System

Over any long journey, we need to do our best to ensure high morale and alignment of the team. This requires everyone to know their own role and goals, and the overall goals of the group.

Many times over the course of the journey, individuals will face independent choices. We want to ensure they have the tools to make the best decisions to advance the group's goals.

The vision is the primary element to achieve this, but we also need to ensure the vision is in balance with other key elements in the navigation system.

As a living organism, an organization must ensure that key elements are in balance and working together. In biology, this is called homeostasis. In our work, we call it harmony. When one part is out of balance, the entire system is disrupted.

The Navigation System

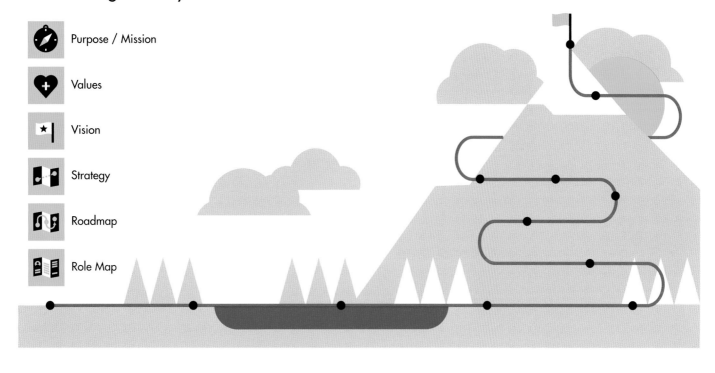

Purpose / Mission

Values

Vision

Strategy

Roadmap

Role Map

The navigation system has at least six parts:

Purpose / Mission

This is your enduring reason for being. It likely changes very little over time. Some organizations call it their purpose and others their mission, but in either case, it's likely the most permanent element of the navigation system. It is, quite simply, the reason the organization exists. All other elements should ladder up to this.

Values

These are your principles or standards of behavior as an organization, and they also change little over time. While the purpose/mission defines what your organization exists to do, the values describe the guardrails of how the organization behaves in the process of doing it. Values may shift and evolve in response to new stimuli, but usually at a very slow pace.

Vision

This is a description of the destination your organization is trying to reach. It should always be in service to the organization's purpose or mission. Your vision describes where you want to be, by when, in pursuit of your mission or purpose. This is a hotly contested topic, but we strongly believe that your vision represents a snapshot in time—your next destination—rather than the ultimate destination of your organization. Otherwise, what would distinguish it from your mission or purpose? Defining a clear vision for where the organization is headed gives the organization a focus point on the horizon so they can advance together to an achievable goal in its pursuit of the mission or purpose.

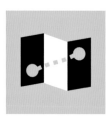

Strategy

Very simply, we define strategy as the plan to achieve the vision. If the vision is where you're going, the strategy is how you plan to get there. The strategy shapes how we organize, resource, and direct our activities, but we know that strategy will likely shift and evolve as we learn new information on the journey.

Roadmap

A roadmap defines the specific steps the organization will take to execute strategy and major milestones along the route. Because we'll need to evolve and adapt as we move forward, the roadmap is very clear in the near term and likely less defined as it moves out. The roadmap defines the next known steps and clarifies people's roles. There may be multiple roadmaps, as different teams may have different roles in the strategy.

Role Map

Whether called a job description, a role map, or something else, the role map defines the roles to execute the roadmap. Not everyone will stand at the summit— many people have a role earlier in the strategy, and each part is necessary to the strategy's overall success. What's critical is that everyone can clearly see the role they play—and why it is important to achieving the vision.

We learned earlier about how people need line of sight for a strategy to be successful. The navigation system is where line of sight comes together. It enables everyone in the organization to connect their role to their team's roadmap and the roadmap to the overall strategy. It also helps them understand how that strategy leads to the vision, and how the vision serves the values, mission, or purpose.

For strategy activation to be successful among thinking human beings and be an effective tool to both persuade them to join the journey and to guide them while on it, we need to ensure that each element of the system is in harmony with the others.

If, for example, the vision conflicts with the values or purpose, it will feel discordant to the people in the organization, and they will reject it. Or if the strategy suggests one thing, but the role map holds people accountable to another, conflict will ensue. Just imagine what would happen if we told people to do things differently but didn't change their financial incentives accordingly or asked them to do something that ran counter to the company's purpose?

Before launching or embarking on any activation journey, we need to audit our navigation system to ensure harmony. If not, the journey may be doomed before we start.

Agility to Sense, Respond, and Adapt

Lastly, as every expedition leader knows, while our initial course may be charted as a straight line from point A to point B, our actual course is almost never a straight line. Along the route, we may need to navigate around an obstacle, stop for needed repairs or new resources, get blown off course by a storm, or divert to take advantage of an unexpected opportunity.

As they say in the military, "No plan survives first contact with the enemy."

So, for activation planning to be successful, we need to remember that change is a constant and anticipate that our plan will need to shift as we advance and learn more. Hence, we should build agility into the plan as a core principle from the start. To do this, we need to build two elements into our program.

First, we include a **measurement system** to help track progress and reveal our position. This has three components:

- **Objectives:** What objectives will define our success? Can we clearly articulate what success looks like and how to know when we've reached each objective?

- **Measures:** How can we measure those objectives, and what are our goals along the route? How much progress towards each objective should we expect to make at key intervals along the route?

- **Feedback loops:** How do we collect and report data to reveal our measures? Are these tracking systems in place today, and if not, what will it take to create them?

Second, we need to include a **governance model** that enables us to make course corrections to keep us moving towards the destination, regardless of what comes up. This should include at least two components:

- **Sense:** What prompts, signals, or insights will tell us when we need to act or course-correct? Do we have a system to "sense" these signals and provide them in a regular cadence to decision-makers?

- **Response:** Who has the authority to convert insights into actions by deciding to change our path? Do we have a structure to provide needed information to respond in a timely manner?

While we start off with a plan, we should anticipate that our actual route won't be a straight line. We should therefore chart a regular series of checkpoints to measure where we are and to identify what's working well and where we need to do better.

With those insights in hand, we should identify and empower an individual or a group to make needed course corrections by converting the insights into action and making corrections to the plan.

Having these two elements in place equips our change program with a guidance system to help it adapt to change and course correct as needed, increasing our chances of successfully reaching our destination as quickly as possible. While we might divert from the planned route, we will always have the vision in mind as our "true north."

Ultimately, agility not only gives us a more realistic approach to executing an achievable plan, but also—by leveraging feedback along the way—accelerates our success.

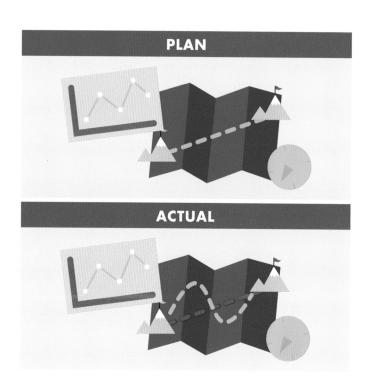

Principles of Modern Change

Before we begin exploring practical approaches to developing a strategy activation program, I'd like to leave you with a set of principles to keep in mind as you embark on the work.

We believe that modern change should be based on principle, not process. It should leverage insights garnered from our understanding of how humans learn, adapt to new information, and develop in new ways.

To develop these insights, we can look to fields like psychology, anthropology, and sociology, and to applied practices like design thinking and human-centered design. These disciplines offer many effective tools to support the acceleration of change adoption in the modern organization, and we can borrow from them to upgrade our approaches to accelerating change.

At XPLANE, we've identified eight such principles that we use in our own work leading change programs with large organizations:

Co-Create

We need to engage the people in the organization in the design of the solution, for their insights and understanding are critical to designing the best solution, and their involvement in the solution will invest them in the adoption of it. We have two sayings that apply here. The first is that the smartest person in the room is the room, and the second is that people support that which they create. The days of consultants who parachute into your organization, do studies and assessments, then throw their proposed solution over the wall are over, as are the days of consultants who act like they're the smartest person in the room. Co-creation is fundamental to effective strategy activation.

Invest in Activation

We need to make activation planning and investment a core element of all strategic planning and change programs. It seems obvious, but it's not to most organizations. We are still stuck in the top-down, command-and-control mindset, which assumes execution is the next step after planning. In the modern world, it's a three-step process: plan, activate, execute. Without an investment of time and resources into the activation phase, our strategy is more likely than not to fail.

Empathize with Stakeholders

To get people on board with change, we need to understand what motivates them and what barriers exist to their adopting new ways of working. Why might they be excited, and why might this change threaten them in some way? If we don't understand the wants and needs of the stakeholders, and the differing needs of different stakeholder groups, we don't stand a chance of effectively activating our teams. This is where empathy comes in. The tools we borrowed from psychology and design thinking help us apply an empathy lens to our work. Empathy helps us figuratively walk in stakeholders' shoes and to understand their wants and needs so we can properly address them.

Visualize the Journey

If you can't draw a map,
you don't know where you're going.
To successfully activate people,
we need to show them clearly what
the destination looks like and how we
plan to get there. And then we need to actually visualize it
by creating a one-page visual or other form of visualization
to help people see—quickly—what you see. Visual
communication accelerates understanding and alignment.

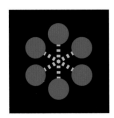

Systemize the Linkages

We need to ensure that the elements
of the change we seek hang together
in harmony. Our vision should be
consistent with our mission or purpose.
Our strategy should explain how we
achieve our vision. Our roadmap, role maps, incentive
plans, and budgets should clearly define what part each
person plays in the overall picture, and how we'll support
them to be successful. If any element of this system is out of
alignment, the entire program could fail, so systemizing the
linkages is a key principle of activation from the start.

Engage Employees

We need to invest extra effort to engage employees at every stage of the process. While some may be deeply involved in the co-creation of possible solutions, for example, others may not have a direct hand in that work. Regardless, everyone should be engaged in feedback loops, peer-to-peer learning, and continuous improvement initiatives.

Embed It in the Organization

The signs and symbols of an organization tell employees what is important to that organization. We therefore need to ensure that our activation program is visible in the conversations, rituals, and physical environment of the organization wherever possible. What are the flagpoles, signposts, gathering places, rituals, events, and billboards in the organization, and how do we ensure our program shows up at each?

Make it Agile

While it's true that no plan survives first contact, that is a secondary argument for why we should build agility into strategy activation programs. The principal reason goes back to biology—to the learning organism. If we have the correct feedback mechanisms in place to learn as we go, we'll be able to sense and respond to issues and opportunities more quickly, pushing resources to where they are needed to accelerate change. Why stick to an expensive communication plan if everyone gets it quickly in the initial awareness phase and wants to learn how to do it? Shift those resources to the learning phase, and use the feedback to learn what people need to learn, tailoring the approach to respond directly to their needs.

By shifting from a process-based approach to one based on principle, and by embracing tools and methods more closely aligned to supporting human growth and development, we can align our change management practices to the needs and realities of the evolved modern organization. In doing so, we improve the organization's capacity for change, accelerating overall change adoption and ultimately our success.

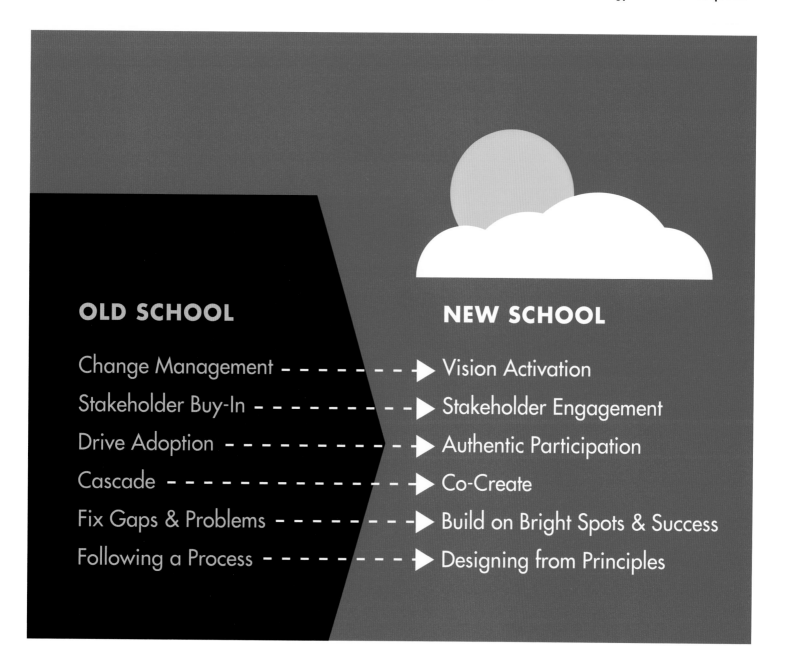

OLD SCHOOL

NEW SCHOOL

Change Management – – – – – – – –▶ Vision Activation

Stakeholder Buy-In – – – – – – – – –▶ Stakeholder Engagement

Drive Adoption – – – – – – – – – – –▶ Authentic Participation

Cascade – – – – – – – – – – – – – –▶ Co-Create

Fix Gaps & Problems – – – – – – – –▶ Build on Bright Spots & Success

Following a Process – – – – – – – – –▶ Designing from Principles

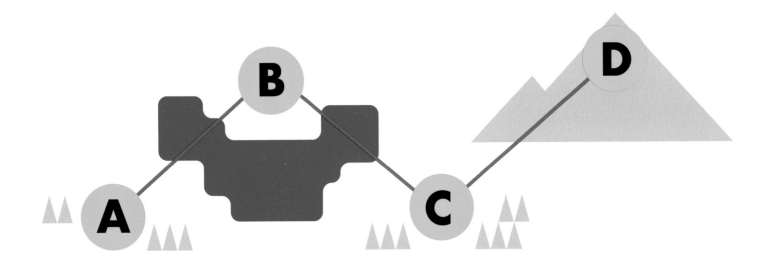

part 5
how to craft a strategy activation program

Phases of a Strategy Activation Program

Now let's shift from theory to practice. With some shared understanding of why strategy activation is important, we now want to equip you with an approach that will help accelerate your vision. In the remaining chapters, we'll share a practical approach, tools, and methods you can use in your daily work leading change.

While strategy activation is less formulaic and more principle-based than traditional change methods, there is a craft to it which can be shared and a basic flow to how the work typically progresses.

That flow carries on the metaphor of leading a journey.
We will break it down into four phases, with steps within them:

Phase 1: Envision

Create a clear and authentic vision that will speak to people's hearts and minds and show them the path to realize it.

In the Envision phase, our focus is on creating a clear vision of the future we're trying to create, the case for change, and the route and measurement system to guide us.

Phase 2: Discover

Map the terrain ahead and barriers to change for stakeholders and the organization.

In the Discover phase, we conduct research and gather insights to understand the stakeholders and their needs, the organization and its capacity for change, and the broader context and the forces working for and against us.

Phase 3: Design

Chart the course ahead to prepare for known and unknown needs.

In the Design phase, we leverage insights we've uncovered and combine a set of building blocks into an activation plan, which provides stakeholders with the communications, learning, and support they need to move up the activation curve.

Phase 4: Execute

Embark on the journey, measure progress along the way, and adapt and refine throughout.

Execution goes beyond launching the program. This phase is all about agility: sensing and responding to changes to keep the program on track. Key activities are development of a governance model, monitoring of a measurement system, and ongoing program refinement.

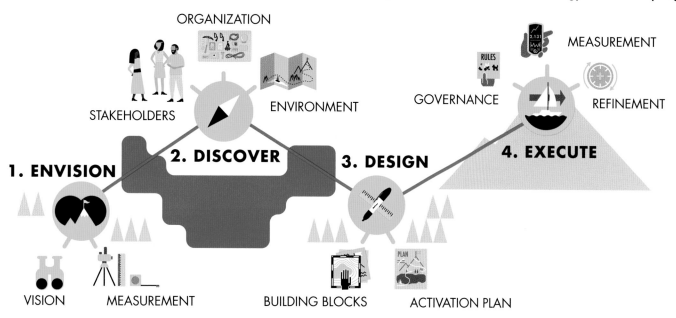

ORGANIZATION

STAKEHOLDERS

ENVIRONMENT

MEASUREMENT

GOVERNANCE

REFINEMENT

2. DISCOVER

1. ENVISION

3. DESIGN

4. EXECUTE

VISION MEASUREMENT

BUILDING BLOCKS

ACTIVATION PLAN

Strategy activation departs from traditional approaches in that it is human-centered, iterative by design, and principle-based.

We develop an approach that's tailored to each stakeholder group and their unique needs. Not all groups will advance at the same pace, and some might iterate and course-correct more frequently than others. By designing our approach from a human-centered perspective, we recognize that the organization is not a machine and that one size won't fit all. To succeed, we need to understand the unique needs of stakeholder groups and develop an approach tailored to meet those needs, while removing barriers to adoption.

We also build in agility from the start with a measurement system and feedback loops which allow us to adapt to new information and course-correct throughout. Leveraging the design thinking approach, we recognize that only through iterative design—a continuous loop of ideation, prototyping, and testing—can the organization move forward consistently, while responding to new barriers and opportunities at each step.

This approach relies more on a series of flexible principles than a rigid process. Success depends less on the order of the steps than how they are taken—in other words, principles matter more than process. Empathy, engagement, co-creation, and agility, applied consistently, generate better results faster than rigidly following a process.

The goal, in the end, is to get everyone to the destination—even if each group takes a slightly different route.

Vision Map

Measurement System

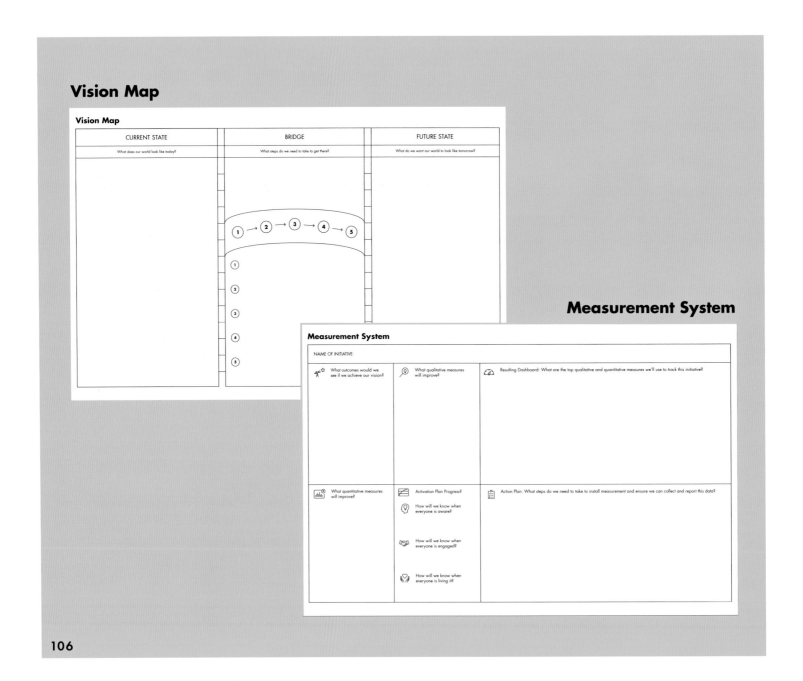

Phase 1: Envision

Create a clear and authentic vision that will speak to people's hearts and minds and show them the path to realize it.

Recall that one of the principal reasons strategies fail is that the people responsible for executing them don't have clear line of sight between their role and the end goal. To succeed in any change, everyone must clearly see the end goal and how they connect to it. Without this clarity and alignment, everyone is moving in multiple different directions—resulting in a loss of energy, focus, and progress.

The Goal

This phase has two goals: to define clearly the vision of our destination and the measures of success so we know where we are and when we've arrived.

Vision: We need to paint a very clear picture of where we're headed, as well as why we're going there. To ensure we provide everyone the line of sight they need, and generate the alignment that we need, a clear vision is elemental.

And by clear vision, we aren't referring to what companies typically call a vision statement. It is literally a picture, a clear map showing the destination and how to get there.

Vision statements may be interpreted differently by different people and lack the depth to create clarity. They might describe the destination—for instance, "we're going to Xanadu"—but they offer very little in telling us what Xanadu looks like, the route to get there, or how to recognize it when we arrive.

Even if ten people know from the company's vision statement that we're going to Xanadu, they probably have ten different images of what Xanadu is and how to get there.

A vision map, however, provides much greater detail and fidelity, reducing the risk of misunderstanding and misalignment. It visually paints a picture of the destination and what it looks like, so all will understand how to recognize success. It also provides information on how to get there so all will coordinate and take the same, agreed-upon path.

And the best vision maps also contain information on why we're going there—the case for change—showing the contrast between our current state and our improved future state. This helps to build motivation and alignment through clear line of sight to the destination.

No vision statement can achieve the depth of shared understanding and alignment that a vision map can provide. Because you can show it to people, they can see more clearly what you see.

Measures

We need to understand what the measures of success are, so we know when we've reached our destination. It also enables us to mark time and distance along the route to evaluate how far we've come and how far we have yet to go.

Once we have a vision map which establishes a clear vision of the destination and the route to get there, it's very important to establish the measurement system right away.

Your measurement system should build upon your vision map by answering the question "What impact will we achieve if we reach our vision, and how can we measure that?"

For example, if your vision is to transform your organization to provide your industry's best customer experience, how could you measure that? Perhaps your industry measures customer experience using the Net Promoter Score (NPS), and the industry performs at a 50 NPS. Perhaps then, your measurement system starts by establishing a 60 NPS as your measure of success. You've established the vision (and

supported it with a visual representation of what that looks like, of course!), and you've set the target to know you've achieved it—a measure of 60 NPS.

Once the target measure is established, you can then define the next elements of your measurement system—milestones and pace.

Milestones are interim goals. Let's say our vision is to achieve 60 NPS in three years. It's clear where we want to be three years from now, but what about in six months, a year, two years? Milestones provide tangible near-term destinations to focus on and a series of achievable next steps, which build momentum towards the final goal with each achievement.

The pace is the rate at which we'll move between milestones. How long will it take to go from our current 50 NPS to 52? Then how long will it take to get to 55? And so on.

We measure pace between milestones, rather than just between start and destination, because pace—especially in change programs—is rarely linear. Although it takes great effort to get a train moving from a dead stop, as it begins to move, it takes less and less energy to build and maintain momentum.

The same is true of most change efforts. While it takes a large effort to increase NPS by two points, the next three points come more easily, and the next five points easier still. As alignment increases and team momentum grows, the impacts are often cumulative.

We establish the measurement system from the very start to infuse our vision with credibility, clarity, and transparency by making sure everyone can clearly see how we're doing along the route.

There are three benefits to this:

First, we'll know what our final goal is and how to determine when we've arrived.

Second, we'll be able to measure progress along the route so we can know if we need to speed up, slow down, or reallocate resources to achieve our destination on time.

Third, a clear measurement system feeds motivation. For sponsors of our expedition—the executive leaders or board of directors, for example—the ability to clearly define, measure, and report progress builds confidence and makes the business case to secure ongoing resources. And for the participants in the expedition—employees, staff, partners—measurement provides feedback on progress, building ongoing motivation and momentum.

The Theory

The power of vision maps is anchored in millennia of experience. Humans are unique in the scope of our ability to establish an objective, secure and combine resources, and collaborate in groups to achieve shared goals.

In the earliest days, we did this to secure resources by hunting or farming, to establish communities, and to discover new destinations and resources. Over time, humans have developed great aptitude for aligning groups to take journeys for a myriad of reasons—exploration, military conquest, improved quality of life, etc.

In almost every case, a map is a central tool in these journeys, serving two basic purposes. One is as a spatial database—a two-dimensional representation of a three-dimensional space. The other is as a communication device.

Sometimes the map was incomplete, and one of the journey's objectives was to fill in the detail. In other cases, the map was clearer, enabling success at an accelerated pace. But in every case, maps have been critical alignment tools to bring people and resources together with an objective.

You can't embark on a journey, or even describe a journey effectively, without a map.

What makes a good map? These are the seven elements of a good map:

Purpose

Every map is based on a purpose. The purpose of a political map is to define territorial boundaries, while the purpose of a physical map is to define the terrain. Some maps may serve multiple purposes, like a topographical map you might take on a hike, which likely shows both boundaries and terrain features—two elements that are valuable to a hiker.

Title

Every map needs a title which clearly communicates its subject matter. This often includes both a description of the purpose and the physical area of focus—for example, "Topographical Map of Xanadu."

Frame

Maps represent space, but not all of space. Instead, a map represents the space defined by a frame—usually a border and a grid—which clearly sets the boundaries of what's included in the map and what is not.

Orientation

Maps include a device or a symbol, such as a compass rose, to indicate the orientation of a map so that it can be aligned relative to your direction of travel.

Scale

The scale indicates the ratio between the distance on the map and the actual distance traveled—for example, one inch on the map equals one mile on the ground.

Legend

Sometimes called a key, the legend describes the meanings of symbols used on the map, allowing meaningful information to be conveyed quickly.

Labels

Labels describe unique features, place names, and other information to help the map be better understood.

And because our goal is to define a clear vision and the route to get there, we need to add some elements to our map to form an effective chart of our journey. Like an expedition leader or a ship captain, we'll begin our work with a good map, and then we'll chart a course on the map, showing clearly where and how we wish to travel.

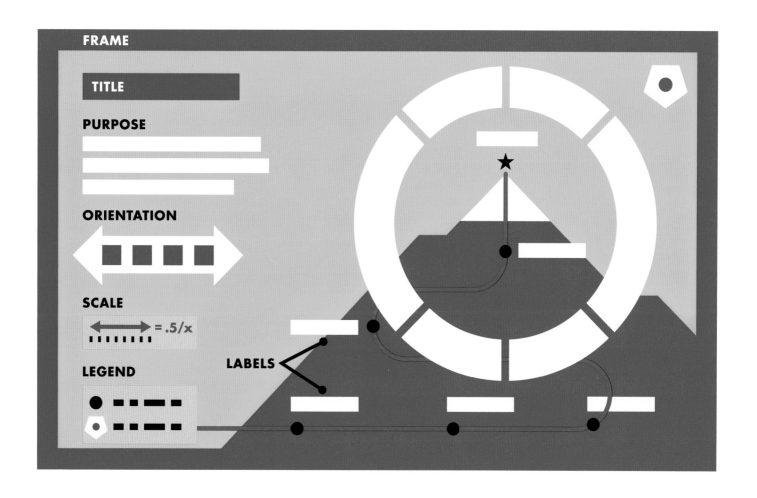

To clearly chart our course, we'll add a few additional elements, including the destination, the route, the milestones, and the measurement system.

Destination: We need to clearly mark the target destination on the map—that place we plan to get to in achievement of our vision. The destination may be marked by a quantitative measurement (such as NPS score or other qualitative metric), or by an outcome or impact we wish to achieve.

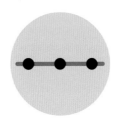

Milestones: Along our route there will be markers that are meaningful to convey—the milestones that tell us when we've reached an interim objective. The area between each pair of milestones is a segment, allowing us to break the overall journey down into more digestible parts that our teams can focus on.

Route: There are many ways to get to a destination, but we'll want to begin the journey with a planned route. Our route is the strategy to reach our destination, visualized as a roadmap from the current location to our destination.

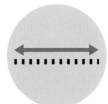

Measurement: We'll want to convey the measurement system that we'll use to mark the pace we expect between the milestones. Often this is depicted as a combination of time and distance: how far will we go and how fast? This communicates to the map reader what is expected in each segment of the journey.

So, to create a clear vision, we combine these: the elements of the map define the terrain of your journey, and the elements of our chart define the route we expect to take and the measurement system we'll use. Together, we have an effective vision map.

The Envision phase is about discovering and synthesizing all of these elements into a clear vision map and measurement system, which provide a firm foundation for our activation program.

We'll want to develop this as an exercise for ourselves first to ensure we have addressed each element and can see it clearly for ourselves. Only then will we be prepared to help others see it as clearly as we do.

Let's explore how we'll do that.

The Practice

We need to exit the Envision phase with two things in hand: a vision map which visually depicts our desired future on a single page, and a measurement system that tells us how far we must go and how we'll know when we're there.

Crafting the Vision: Regardless of the scale of your vision—whether it's a small team initiative or an enterprise-wide transformation—you can create an initial draft of your vision map by answering these six questions:

1. **Who is the vision holder?** A *vision holder* is whoever sees the desired future most clearly. A vision map requires an author or group of authors who can see farther than the others. Begin by identifying the vision holders—they are the creators of this first draft.

2. **What is the case for change?** To embark on a new journey, there is usually a catalyst that triggers your desire to change. This is the fork in the road that—when described—will create momentum for exploration of a new route. This could be an external force, like a competitor's action or a change in the environmental context, or an internal force, like the loss or gain of a powerful capability.

3. **What is the current state?** Your current state is the point of departure for your journey. It describes the status quo—good or bad—and how it doesn't satisfy the organization's needs.

4. **What is the desired future state?** This is the point of arrival: what the desired future looks like and why it better satisfies the case for change than the status quo.

5. **What's the best-guess roadmap?** While there's a lot more planning to do, at this point you need at least a broad sense of how to get from the current state to the future state. This roadmap begins to outline your strategy and gives comfort that the route is potentially achievable.

6. **What are the impacts and outcomes?** We need to understand and catalog the differences between where we are and our desired destination, both to persuade others that the journey is worth taking and to measure progress and know when we have arrived at our destination.

To embark on a new journey, there is usually a catalyst that triggers your desire to change. This is the fork in the road that—when described— will create momentum for exploration of a new route.

The answers to these six questions contain everything you need to create your first vision map. To support this process, here's a worksheet to create your own:

This worksheet can serve as a literal or inspirational template for a vision mapping exercise. You can print it out and complete it individually, but if you are working as a group, you will want to use a sheet of paper, a digital collaboration space, or a whiteboard to sketch your vision.

The act of sketching—no matter your skill level—is a visual thinking exercise which accelerates understanding by helping people see the ideas in your head.

Here's how you do it:

1. Divide the page or whiteboard into three sections. Label the top of the sections with Current State, Bridge, and Future State.

2. If there are multiple participants, start by having each one complete the exercise individually on their own page.

3. Invite participants to draw a sketch of the current state: What does today's situation look like?

4. Then invite them to draw a sketch of the future state: What do they want the situation to look like in the future?

5. With both states drawn, ask the participants to complete the Bridge section by identifying specific actions to take or things to change for the future state to be realized.

6. If there are multiple participants, have each share their vision with the group, then discuss similarities and differences and identify common themes. These themes become common ground for further exploration.

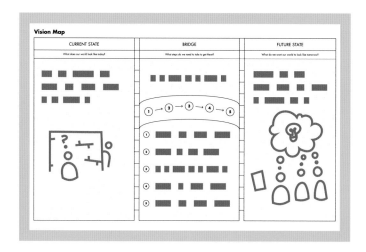

While the initial draft may be rough—sketches, captions, and sticky notes—the important thing at this stage is to get the essential information on one page.

The one-page constraint helps you to focus on the essence of the story, for that's what a vision map is: a visual narrative of a better future to persuade others to follow you there. The one-page limit forces you to boil the narrative down to its essence, making it clearer both to you and your audience.

From here, you can refine it to the degree of fidelity that you require. For some, that's a whiteboard sketch that can be drawn live in every meeting, while for others it's a fully illustrated brand-appropriate vision mural on the wall. The most important thing is to keep it visual, which helps people embed that picture in their minds.

Vision Map

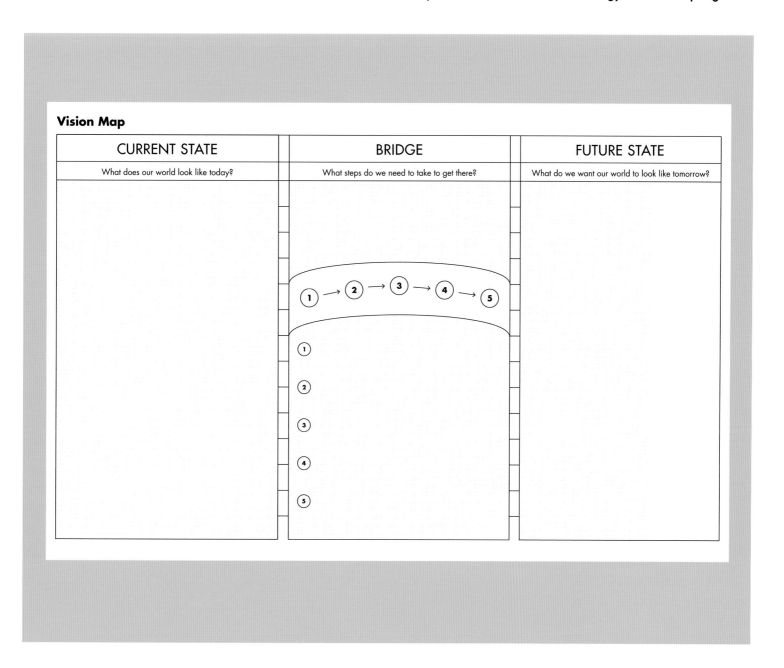

CURRENT STATE	BRIDGE	FUTURE STATE
What does our world look like today?	What steps do we need to take to get there?	What do we want our world to look like tomorrow?

Developing the Measurement System

Our next step is to add a measurement system to our map by answering three questions:

1. **What are the most important outcomes or impacts?**
    Of all the potential outcomes and impacts of achieving our vision, pick three to five that are most important or will resonate most with stakeholders. It's hard to get people to track a dashboard of ten key performance indicators (KPIs), but if they can focus on three things, they're more likely to achieve them.

2. **What are the best ways to measure each?** Identify the best way of measuring each objective. Some measures may be easily measured with numbers, such as a financial goal or customer satisfaction score. Others may be subjective measures about people's feelings or perceptions, such as brand preference or culture alignment. Both qualitative and quantitative measures are valid, but each outcome will be better measured by one or the other.

3. **How will we know when we've reached our goals?**
    Establish a target goal which tells us when we've reached the vision. Is there a quantitative or qualitative measure that will signal we've arrived? We may embark on a new journey towards another destination, but first we want to know when we've completed this one.

The answers to these questions provide enough information to develop our initial measurement system, including a dashboard that we can leverage to communicate progress throughout the initiative.

Here's a worksheet to help develop a dashboard for your measurement system:

Instructions for use:

1. Refer to your vision map for the key outcomes that you would expect to see when the vision is achieved.

2. Document both quantitative and qualitative measures and goals.

3. Add a measure to track movement along the activation curve: one each for the Hear It, Believe It, and Live It phases.

    This may be accomplished using a survey question to measure your goal for each phase. For example, on a scale of 1–5, with one being "strongly disagree" and 5 being "strongly agree," what percentage of employees surveyed agree with each of the following:

    »   I am aware of and understand our vision and strategy.

    »   I am actively working to support and execute our strategy in my daily work.

    »   We are living our vision and strategy today.

4. Select the top measures to include on your dashboard.

5. If these measures are not already in place, develop an action plan to install the measurement system in your organization.

The Product: Draft Dashboard

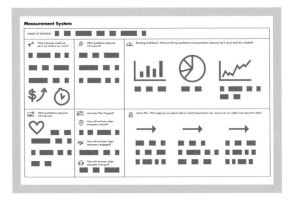

Measurement System

NAME OF INITIATIVE:

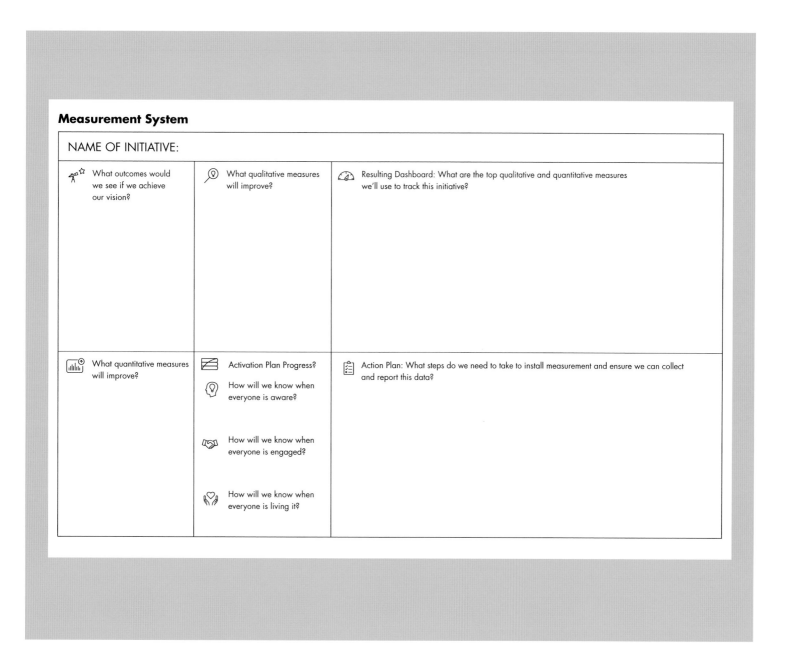

What outcomes would we see if we achieve our vision?

What qualitative measures will improve?

Resulting Dashboard: What are the top qualitative and quantitative measures we'll use to track this initiative?

What quantitative measures will improve?

Activation Plan Progress?

How will we know when everyone is aware?

How will we know when everyone is engaged?

How will we know when everyone is living it?

Action Plan: What steps do we need to take to install measurement and ensure we can collect and report this data?

The Envision phase is complete when you have a Vision Map in hand that you could bring to a meeting to help an individual or a group see your vision clearly. Because you've also developed a draft dashboard, you'll also be able to help people understand the goals, and the definition of success. In combination, these two products give you what you need to launch your journey.

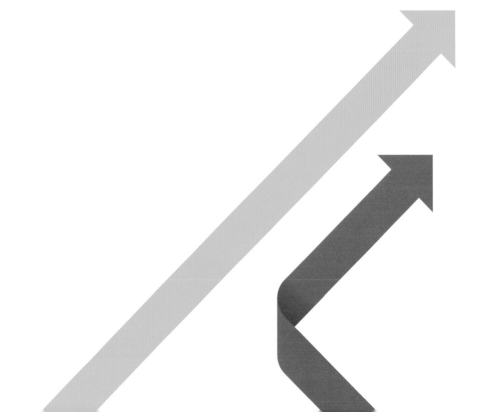

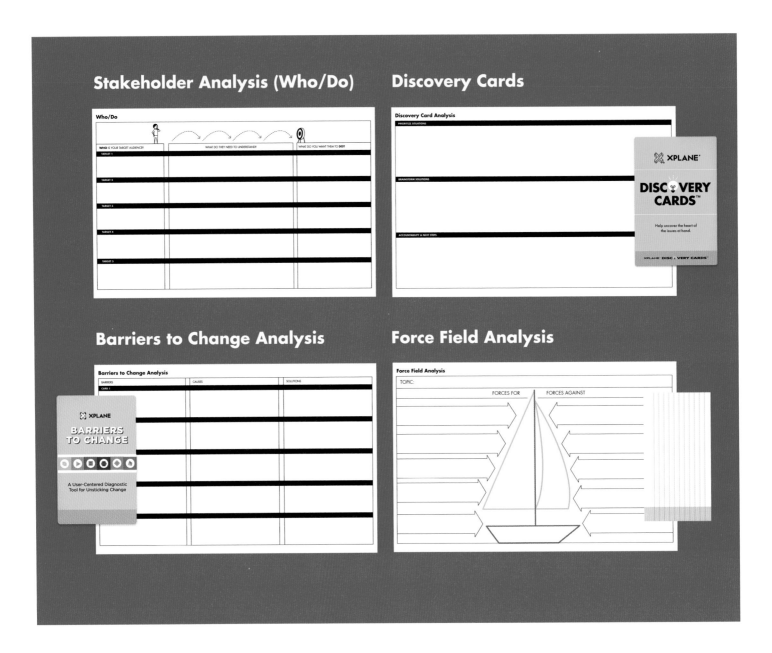

Stakeholder Analysis (Who/Do)

Who/Do

WHO IS YOUR TARGET AUDIENCE?	WHAT DO THEY NEED TO UNDERSTAND	WHAT DO YOU WANT THEM TO DO?
TARGET 1		
TARGET 2		
TARGET 3		
TARGET 4		
TARGET 5		

Discovery Cards

Discovery Card Analysis

PRIORITIZE SITUATIONS

BRAINSTORM SOLUTIONS

ACCOUNTABILITY & NEXT STEPS

XPLANE

DISCOVERY CARDS™

Help uncover the heart of the issues at hand.

XPLANE DISCOVERY CARDS™

Barriers to Change Analysis

Barriers to Change Analysis

BARRIERS	CAUSES	SOLUTIONS
CARD 1		

XPLANE

BARRIERS TO CHANGE

A User-Centered Diagnostic Tool for Unsticking Change

Force Field Analysis

Force Field Analysis

TOPIC:

FORCES FOR   FORCES AGAINST

Phase 2: Discover

Map the terrain ahead and barriers to change for stakeholders and the organization.

The Goal

The goal of this phase is to learn as much as we can about the route ahead and to use that information to address obstacles and opportunities with our teams.

While some journeys go into the uncharted wild with little to no knowledge of what's ahead, that's a very rare purpose for an organizational journey. In almost every example of an organizational transformation, there is a lot of information available about the terrain ahead, the potential obstacles, and the shortcuts that might exist.

Most of this information is in the heads of the people you plan to bring with you on the journey. While neither you nor any of them can see the entire picture as individuals, collectively you can develop a pretty good map of the terrain ahead and use it to chart a better course.

Sadly, this phase is often overlooked and hard to get organizations to invest in. And yet it provides crucial information to influence the outcome of your activation program.

In the real world, if two teams had the same destination, but one was equipped with a rough sketch and the other with a detailed map outlining every obstacle and shortcut, plus tools for the journey, which do you think would succeed first?

As a leader, you must insist on doing the work of discovery. A small investment by a few, early in the process, will yield significant impact when you ask the many to move forward.

Do you recall that employee engagement is one of the primary reasons strategies fail? Well, this is the stage where that failure can be reversed by leveraging the knowledge of key stakeholders and engaging them in the process of mapping the terrain and refining the plans.

The Theory

Before we plan our journey, we need to understand what lies ahead. If people are united in the desire to change, then the organization is quick to adopt changes, the changes will help the organization to thrive, and the investment in an activation program will be much smaller.

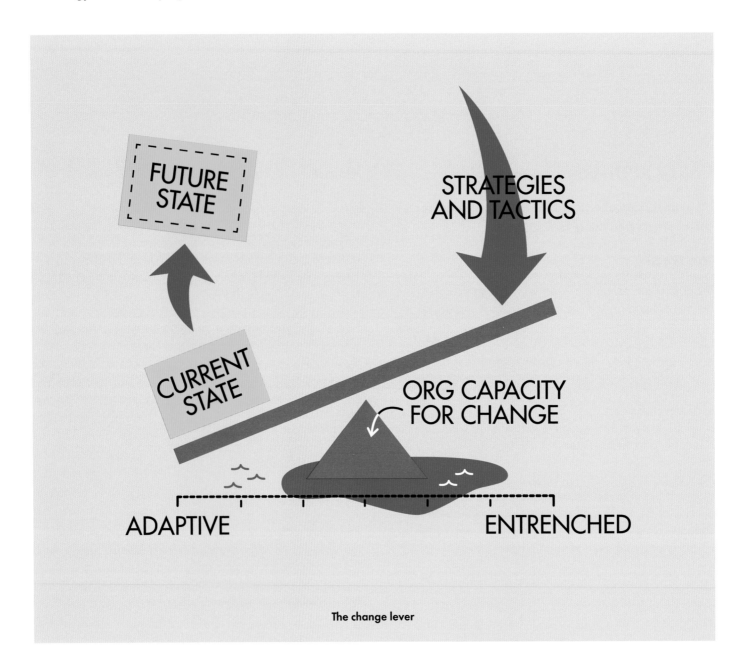

The change lever

However, if people don't understand the case for change, if the organization is resistant and slow to adopt, or if the external environment presents headwinds to slow change adoption, a much greater investment is required.

Hence, the size of the change isn't the only factor in determining the investment required to activate change. The organization's collective adaptability to change also influences how much investment or pressure must be applied to shift it from the current state to the desired one.

We illustrate this with a framework called the *change lever* (see image opposite).

If you think of a seesaw, you'll understand the basic mechanics of the change lever. The distance between our current state and the future state is often measured with gap analysis, which tells us how far we need to go and how much pressure must be applied to move from point A to point B.

This is typically where classic consulting and management theory stop. They identify the current state, define the future state, perform gap analysis, and determine the roadmap of steps and effort required to shift the lever.

However, this approach misses a critical factor: Where is the fulcrum on our seesaw?

Regardless of the size of the gap, if you move the fulcrum of the seesaw closer to the left, less pressure is required to close it. Likewise, if you move it to the right, significantly more pressure is required to close the same gap.

The fulcrum in this model represents the organizational context: the stakeholders, the organization itself, and the surrounding context.

With a highly adaptive organization and supportive context, often the fulcrum can be moved to the left so that less effort is required to achieve the change. But with a change-resistant organization and context, the fulcrum may actually be to the right of where you imagine it, meaning that significantly more pressure must be applied to achieve your desired change.

This is the very heart of why tailored strategy activation is necessary. If you ignore the reality of the fulcrum, you won't make the required investment to achieve your goals, and your strategy will likely fail.

So the point of the Discover phase is to properly assess the organizational context: How adaptive or resistant is our organization, and how does that inform the size and scope of the activation plan?

125

Having a clear understanding of the context helps us to properly prepare for the type and size of change program to design. We seek to uncover both opportunities and barriers so we can recognize both shortcuts to our destination and obstacles to go around or remove.

We want to map the terrain in three dimensions:

1. **Stakeholders:** Who are the primary groups of stakeholders that need to be aligned and moving forward together for us to succeed? What do we want each of them to do differently than they do today? What are each of these stakeholders' unique wants and needs that must be addressed for them to join our effort?

2. **Organization:** How adaptive to change is the organization? How will its culture, norms, and behaviors impact our efforts? How will it react to the specific change we're seeking to make?

3. **Outside world:** What's happening beyond the walls of our organization to accelerate or impede our efforts?

We then gather our findings into insights in order to convert insights into actions:

1. **Assess the organization's overall capacity for change.** Is the organization highly adaptive to change or deeply entrenched, and what does that indicate about the overall size and scope of the activation plan required?

2. **Update the vision map with course corrections resulting from these insights.** For example, will it take more or less time? Do we need to alter the route or roadmap? Do we need to tailor the messaging or narrative?

3. **Catalog findings for the next stage:**

    »   What are the key communications needs for each stakeholder group?

    »   What are the key learning, development, or support needs for each group?

    »   What are the principal risks, and how can we mitigate them?

With these insights, you will then have the information you will need to revise your vision map and measurement system with new inputs to improve your draft from the Envision phase. And you'll have a solid base of insights to shape the outcomes of your next phase of work: design.

The product of this stage is an insights report summarizing what you have discovered. You'll refer to it throughout the effort, not only in the Design phase, but also in crafting messaging during the program itself.

The Practice

The Discover phase utilizes tools borrowed from disciplines discussed earlier in this book:

- **Psychology:** We'll look at the motivations of our stakeholders and their wants and needs, which may influence their willingness to engage in new ways of working

- **Anthropology:** We'll analyze the culture, norms, and behaviors of the group to identify barriers to change and opportunities for acceleration

- **Design thinking:** We'll borrow tools of observation and discovery to help us better understand the underlying mechanics of the system

- **Visual thinking:** We'll shape those tools into user-friendly, engaging exercises to deliver better insights faster than traditional research methods

The products of this phase are key insights about stakeholders, organization, and the outside world. Let's look at our approach to each in turn, with some tools to accelerate understanding.

The Stakeholders

While our change effort may impact the entire organization, a handful of stakeholder groups are critical to get on board. These are the make-or-break groups on whom success hinges. For example, if we're implementing a customer-centricity transformation, we need everyone to learn new ways of working, but it's critical to start with people in customer-facing roles, like sales, customer service, and service delivery. Importantly, the needs of these three groups may be very different, so we need to understand each group intimately.

We need to answer three questions about our stakeholders:

1. Who are the key stakeholder groups that we need aligned and moving forward together to be successful?

2. What do we want each of them to do differently than they do today?

3. What are these stakeholders' unique wants and needs that must be addressed for them to join our effort?

There are many ways to map the stakeholders in an organization, including interviews, focus groups, and brainstorming exercises. But to develop the depth of understanding required to surface their wants and needs, we suggest the use of two tools: the Empathy Map and the Who/Do Canvas.

Let's start with the Empathy Map:

The Empathy Map helps us get inside the head of each type of stakeholder and "walk in their shoes." Not only does it help us understand attitudes towards the change initiative, but also what may be needed for them to move forward.

Instructions for use:

1. Begin by brainstorming a list of key stakeholder groups that need to be on board for the change effort to be successful. You'll probably come up with a long list.

2. Narrow this list down to the top five to ten groups.

3. For each one, complete an Empathy Map. Working around the canvas, complete each of these areas:

   » Begin by naming the stakeholder (e.g. "Customer Service Representative").

   » Identify what we need them to do to successfully implement change (e.g. "Adopt new, more customer-centric ways of working").

   » Describe what they are seeing, saying, doing, and hearing, as well as what they are likely thinking and feeling today, with special attention on pains in the current state and potential gains in the future state.

4. Once you've completed the map for each stakeholder group, compare them. Some will be very different—unique stakeholder groups should be treated as such, while others with similar profiles can possibly be combined.

5. Review your list of stakeholder groups to ensure you haven't missed any. If you have, complete additional Empathy Maps.

The Product: Empathy Maps for Each Stakeholder

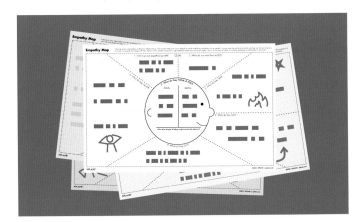

Empathy Map

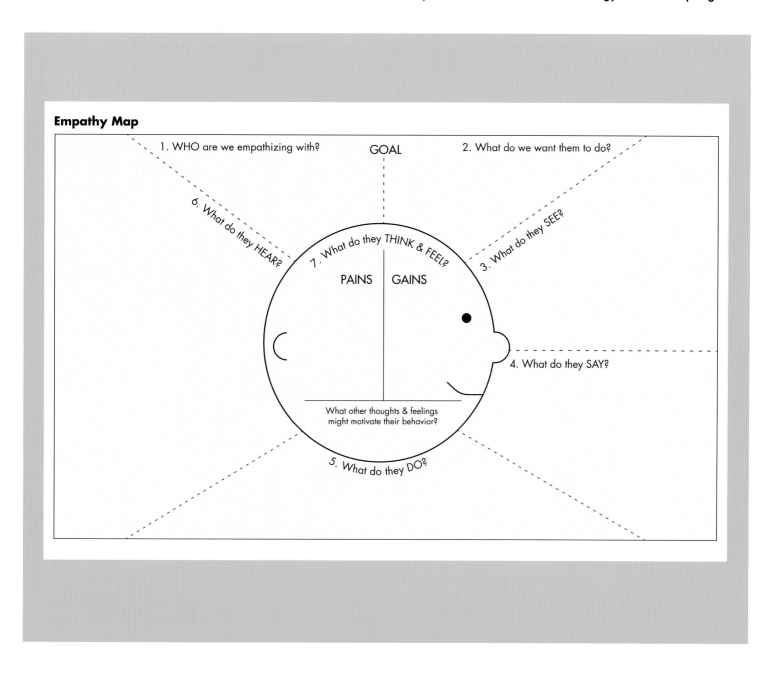

1. WHO are we empathizing with?

GOAL

2. What do we want them to do?

6. What do they HEAR?

3. What do they SEE?

7. What do they THINK & FEEL?

PAINS | GAINS

What other thoughts & feelings might motivate their behavior?

4. What do they SAY?

5. What do they DO?

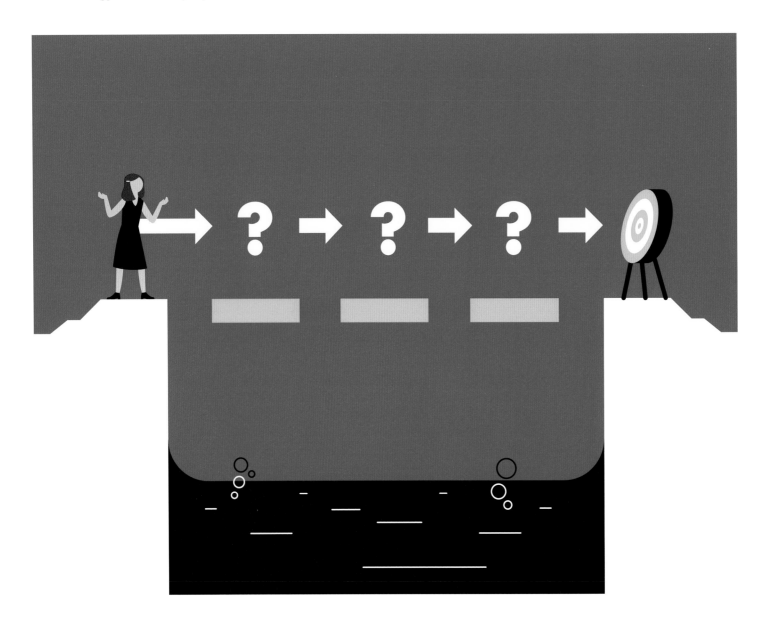

Now, with insight into the wants and needs of key stakeholder groups, we'll utilize the Who/Do Canvas to understand how to tailor our program to meet their unique needs.

The mechanics of the Who/Do Canvas are simple. For each stakeholder group, we'll catalog what we need from them for our change to succeed and which key questions must be addressed to get them on board. For example, our customer service rep (our "Who") may be open to, perhaps even excited about, a more customer-centric approach (our "Change"). They may be willing, therefore, to adopt new ways of working in a more customer-centric way (our "Do").

However, before they can do what we need from them, we'll need to address questions they may have. For example:

- Will you provide the training I need to do things differently?

- Will you change my incentives so I'm rewarded for this new behavior?

- How are we changing other areas of the business that impact the customer experience before they get to me?

We call these questions the understanding chain, as they describe key information people need to understand before they are willing to move to action. The Empathy Maps you created for each stakeholder group are the key to unlocking the understanding chain, as they point to key issues and opportunities for each stakeholder.

Of course, you can deepen your understanding of stakeholder needs by validating the Empathy Map exercise with stakeholder interviews to be sure you have an accurate picture of what sits between the "Who" and the "Do."

Use this understanding to complete the Who/Do worksheet:

Instructions for use:

1. In the Who column, list key stakeholder groups.

2. In the corresponding Do column, list what you want each stakeholder group to do.

3. In each row, document the top three questions you'll need to address before those stakeholders will move to action. Validate your assumptions with research if needed.

4. Compare your results and consolidate any stakeholder groups with very similar questions and Do statements.

5. Review to ensure you haven't missed critical stakeholder groups, and add them if needed.

You now have a catalog of key stakeholder groups and their differing needs. You can typically see at a glance that each group has different requirements. One group may need a heavy dose of communication about the why of the change to get them on board, while another may be aligned with the goal but concerned about training and development to make the change successfully. Another group may be most concerned about the need for new capabilities or technology.

All this paints a picture of how to move each group up the activation curve with the right targeted interventions.

Who/Do

WHO IS YOUR TARGET AUDIENCE?	WHAT DO THEY NEED TO UNDERSTAND?	WHAT DO YOU WANT THEM TO DO?
TARGET 1		
TARGET 2		
TARGET 3		
TARGET 4		
TARGET 5		

The Organization

The second area of inquiry in the Discover phase is an exploration of the organization's culture and its capacity for change. We need to know where to place the organization on the change lever: Is this a highly adaptive organization open to change, or a highly entrenched organization resistant to change? The answer informs how much to invest in activation activities.

We need to answer three key questions about the organization:

- How will its culture, norms, and behaviors impact our efforts?

- How will it react to the specific change we're seeking to make?

- How adaptive to change is the organization?

Understanding what's happening in the organization requires some degree of field research. It's rare that leaders in an organization can correctly assess the complexity and nuance of an organization's potential barriers to change. Often there are blind spots which keep us from seeing all of the potential issues in various pockets of the organization.

Even if your time and budget are limited, we recommend you do some direct research with a cross-section of key stakeholders from the last step. Here are three relatively quick methods to understand the inner workings of the organization and its attitude towards the proposed change (we'll provide more info on these later in the chapter).

1. **Focus groups:** Groups of five to eight representatives of your targeted stakeholder groups can reveal issues and opportunities through facilitated discussion based on a short list of questions.

2. **Card-sort exercises:** These can be used either individually or in groups to surface specific responses to a change effort using cards with descriptors of organizational culture and expected barriers to change. You can produce your own card-sort exercise using index cards or use pre-made products like XPLANE's Discovery Cards.

3. **Workshops:** A workshop format can provide the insights of a focus group with the engagement of an activation program by asking people to not only highlight issues but also brainstorm possible solutions. A workshop is most successful when it goes beyond a simple discussion and introduces exercises into the agenda.

Beyond these techniques, there are two tools that we often use in this phase which you could include in your own toolkit: the Rose/Thorn/Bud exercise and the Eight Dimensions worksheet. Both are effective examples of exercises you might include in a workshop to generate engagement and co-create possible solutions.

First, let's look at the Rose/Thorn/Bud exercise:

Instructions for use:

1. In an in-person workshop, this worksheet can be drawn on a whiteboard and participants can add their ideas using sticky notes. Alternatively, the exercise can be conducted individually using printed worksheets, or online using a collaboration tool like MURAL or Miro.

2. Describe the proposed change at the top.

3. First, ask participants to list roses: things perceived as benefits or positive outcomes of the proposed change.

4. Next, ask participants to list thorns: things perceived as negative about the proposed change.

5. Finally, after a brief discussion of both the roses and thorns, invite the participants to brainstorm possible buds: ideas about helping the change to be successful.

This exercise encourages participants to look at the change from many angles on behalf of the organization, allowing them to reveal both personal points of view and expectations of how the broader organization might react. In addition, this exercise invites them to contribute ideas on how to nurture the change—building engagement while surfacing useful ideas for your change program.

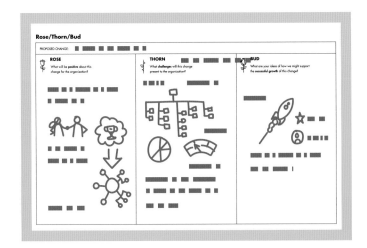

Rose/Thorn/Bud

PROPOSED CHANGE:

🌹 ROSE
What will be **positive** about this change for the organization?

🥀 THORN
What **challenges** will this change present to the organization?

🌷 BUD
What are your ideas of how we might support the **successful growth** of this change?

Next let's look again at the Eight Dimensions, and how the worksheet is used in this phase:

To understand how the organization will react to the change, we use the Eight Dimensions worksheet to analyze potential system impacts. This can be a foundational exercise in a group workshop or an individual exercise.

Instructions for use:

There are three steps:

1. Identify the area or areas of your planned change and note the change in the corresponding area.

2. Evaluate other dimensions that could be impacted by your planned change. One by one, ask yourself if the other seven dimensions will require a corresponding shift to support the change you want to make. Give each one a grade from 1 to 5, with 1 for a little impact and 5 for a significant impact.

3. In areas that will be impacted, list shifts needed to ensure the system is balanced properly.

This analysis helps us see at a systemic level where there are potential pitfalls and barriers to change, which need to be anticipated and mitigated before we launch our activation program.

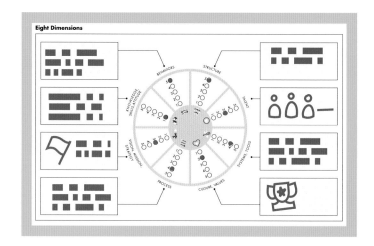

Eight Dimensions

Eight Dimensions

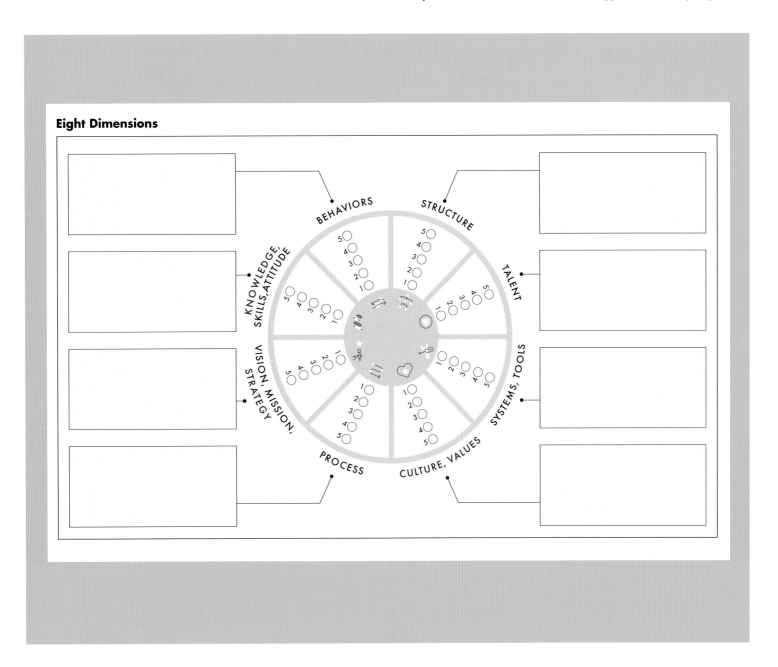

The Outside World

Having looked at the stakeholders and organization, our last discovery focus is an assessment of potential barriers to change in the world outside of the organization.

To develop a clear picture of the environment in which our organization lives and the forces acting on it that are beyond our control, we need to address two key questions:

1. Which external forces could support or accelerate our efforts?

2. Which external forces could threaten or impede our efforts?

For this assessment, we rely on a method called force field analysis, which is a simple and visual way to catalog external forces acting on our organization and their perceived relative power:

Instructions for use:

1. In an in-person workshop, this worksheet can be drawn on a whiteboard, and participants can add their ideas using sticky notes. Alternatively, the exercise can be conducted individually using printed worksheets or online using a collaboration tool like MURAL or Miro.

2. On the left side, have participants brainstorm forces that are working for us: "tailwinds," which will accelerate our success. Group like ideas together and order them from strongest forces at the top to weakest at the bottom.

3. On the right side, have participants brainstorm forces that are working against us: "headwinds," which will slow our advance. Group like ideas together and order them from strongest forces at the top to weakest at the bottom.

4. Discuss the results, making sure all important forces are included and relative strengths are depicted accurately, and revise as needed.

Force field analysis provides a useful picture of external factors to include in planning. For the forces working *for us*, we might explore how to leverage them to accelerate our program, while for those working *against us*, we should discuss how to mitigate risks within our plan.

Remember, these forces impact each organization differently relative to their target. For example, the pandemic was an enormous threat to our clients in the travel industry but an incredible accelerator to another in remote meeting technology—enabling them to dramatically reshape activation plans to go much faster than originally planned.

Collectively, this research to understand stakeholders, organization, and outside forces yields powerful insights to influence your plan and improve its chances of success. The practices above provide a basic toolkit for the essential work required of this phase, with a greater investment yielding greater results.

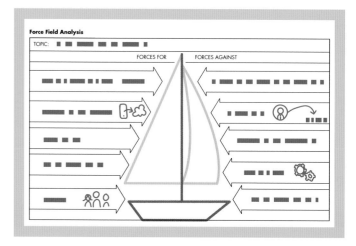

Force Field Analysis

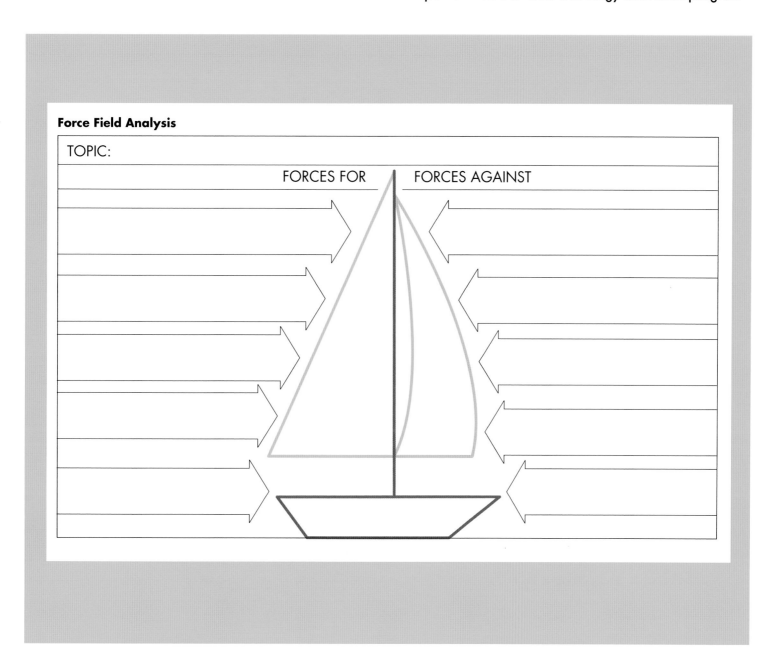

TOPIC:

FORCES FOR FORCES AGAINST

Tools for Insight Generation

Often, one area of exploration may be clear, while another reveals that more research will be required to truly understand what's happening. In this case, there are additional tools and methods for advanced insight generation, evaluation of an organization's capacity for change, and discovery of specific barriers to change.

There are five core toolkits we utilize in insight generation, three of which we've briefly touched upon as well as two additional approaches:

Structured interviews

Gather insights from individual representatives of stakeholder groups

A single interview may give you a biased view of the truth, but a series of short interviews with a representative group of stakeholders will reveal patterns and provide deeper insights into that group's issues and opportunities.

A useful practice is to develop five or six probing questions, set up a group of individual 30 minute interviews, and document answers on sticky notes or in digital notes. After the interviews, you can make an affinity map, grouping answers to each question to reveal common themes.

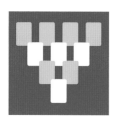

Card-sort exercises

Use cards populated with prompts to uncover consistent themes across a targeted group

Focus groups and workshops

Create structured discovery events to gather insights from targeted stakeholder groups

Fun and engaging, card-sort exercises are a great way to quickly gather information and reveal themes. You can easily create cards using a blank stack of index cards. It's a great 80/20 tool—uncovering 80 percent of the truth in 20 percent of the time of other research methods. You can use discoveries from a card sort to guide deeper insight gathering using one of the other methods.

Card sorts work by having participants sort cards which are pre-populated with prompts into "hits" and "misses." For instance, you might create a deck with a list of behaviors, and have participants identify which are most and least typical in the organization. After only a handful of card-sorts with different stakeholder groups, patterns begin to emerge which reveal the culture of that organization.

Engage stakeholders directly in the discovery process by gathering them together to share and discuss insights and recommendations. Workshops of this type not only surface insights, but provide a forum to explore those insights more deeply as participants reveal the impacts and opportunities that surround them.

It's best to keep focus groups and workshops smaller to foster deeper discussion, so we recommend developing a standard agenda and conducting it as many times as needed in groups of no more than five to ten.

Surveys and assessments

Develop tailored surveys or assessments to quantify trends across large populations

A comprehensive survey of your entire stakeholder population is highly beneficial. For instance, at the start of a major initiative it's important to establish a baseline measurement of your current state—such as the level of employee engagement—to compare your progress throughout the program against that baseline.

Surveys are also beneficial in revealing hidden pockets of truth—trends or insights that might get overlooked in a small-sample method like a card sort or focus group. Here's an example from my own company: though XPLANE consistently earned high Great Place to Work scores, the survey revealed a statistically significant difference in experience based on gender, leading us to deepen our focus and accelerate actions to close that gap.

For benchmark surveys, we recommend finding a partner with credible domain experience to conduct surveys and provide comparative results from other companies. For example, in XPLANE's culture and employee engagement projects, we work with the Great Place to Work Institute. They are an independent third party, which gives employees a higher degree of trust and safety in answering questions honestly. They also provide results with comparisons to benchmark companies of similar sizes in similar industries, which deepens our ability to identify important organizational gaps and opportunities and to measure how we compare to peers.

To solicit ideas or gather feedback, it's never been easier to build, deploy, and tabulate survey results using free or low-cost web-based tools.

You still need to do your homework to understand the mechanics of good survey design, or engage a specialist to help you. But the cost of using surveys during discovery and as an ongoing measurement tool is no longer prohibitive. It can provide deep and revealing insights quickly and economically.

Observation

Observe people without engaging them directly

As anthropologist Margaret Mead once said, "What people say, what people do, and what people say they do are entirely different things."[1]

Observation is a powerful way to gather information as a primary source, rather than by relying on the reported truths of stakeholders. It can be used both to validate gathered insights and to develop new insights overlooked by the stakeholders themselves.

In activation work, we use observation primarily to understand the environment of the organization, the intersections where people meet, and where and how they get and exchange information.

As a change leader, we may not be able to dive deeply into ethnographic practices, relying instead on trained experts. But we can be keen observers and include observations of how things actually work in our insights.

Walk around. Observe where people gather. These may be prime locations for activation communications. Observe where they get information: Is it principally through manager meetings, the grapevine, video monitors on office walls, an annual conference? Each of these should be considered in activation program design.

Understand how some groups exist in one type of environment and others in something quite different. Employees in an office-based environment have a very different context than employees in a manufacturing facility, a field site, or a home office—you'll need to understand and adapt to each of these if you are going to reach them all.

For example, XPLANE led a strategy activation program for a major oil company. In the corporate offices, there were video monitors and well-established digital communication channels to share key messages. But we also had to reach workers on the North Slope of Alaska, who typically worked 14 twelve-hour days in a row, and only rarely gathered in one place—typically the dining hall.

Some observation resulted in a decidedly low-tech but highly effective messaging tool: a "table tent" placed strategically near the condiments on every dining table. Not only did the messages reach our audience, but they were also actively discussed over many meals, with awareness and recall among the highest in the company.

The question of how much discovery is enough is often a function of time and budget, but the insights gathered in this phase are without doubt the most impactful on the success of the activation program. At a minimum, you should know each stakeholder group's wants, needs, and fears, plus the primary communication channels in their working environment.

Create the Insights Report

The final step in the Discover phase is to synthesize the insights you've gathered and convert them into recommended actions.

We recommend that you document your insights and recommendations in an *insights report*. This report serves two purposes: First, to guide the activation program by identifying key points of focus and leverage for each stakeholder group. Second, to provide evidence as to why you recommend these actions and messages, which helps to build momentum and support for your program.

As a starting point for your insights report, use this worksheet to develop a one-page summary of key findings:

Instructions for use:

1. Review the body of your research and select the most important insights to use in shaping the activation plan.

2. In the upper left quadrant, list and prioritize key themes to address for core stakeholder groups ("Stakeholder Insights").

3. In the upper right quadrant, list and prioritize important insights generated from the organizational assessment ("Organization Insights").

4. In the lower left quadrant, list and prioritize key insights from the force field analysis ("Contextual Insights").

5. In the lower right quadrant, list and prioritize recommended actions ("Actions to Take").

The Discover phase is complete when you have a completed insights report to provide your team with the knowledge they need about the terrain ahead, key barriers and opportunities to change, and initial recommendations about how to navigate the journey.

As was mentioned at the start of this chapter, this phase is often the most under-resourced part of the process. But in our experience, it yields the most impactful results. You can use the insights report throughout the remaining phases to inform everything from the overall design of the activation plan to specific messaging and learning objectives.

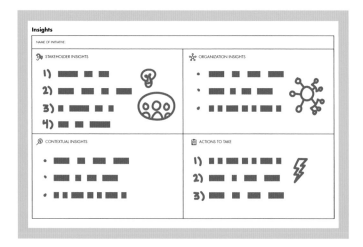

Insights

NAME OF INITIATIVE:	
𓂃 STAKEHOLDER INSIGHTS	⁂ ORGANIZATION INSIGHTS
⊙ CONTEXTUAL INSIGHTS	🗒 ACTIONS TO TAKE

Building Blocks Cheat Sheet

Refinement Punchlist

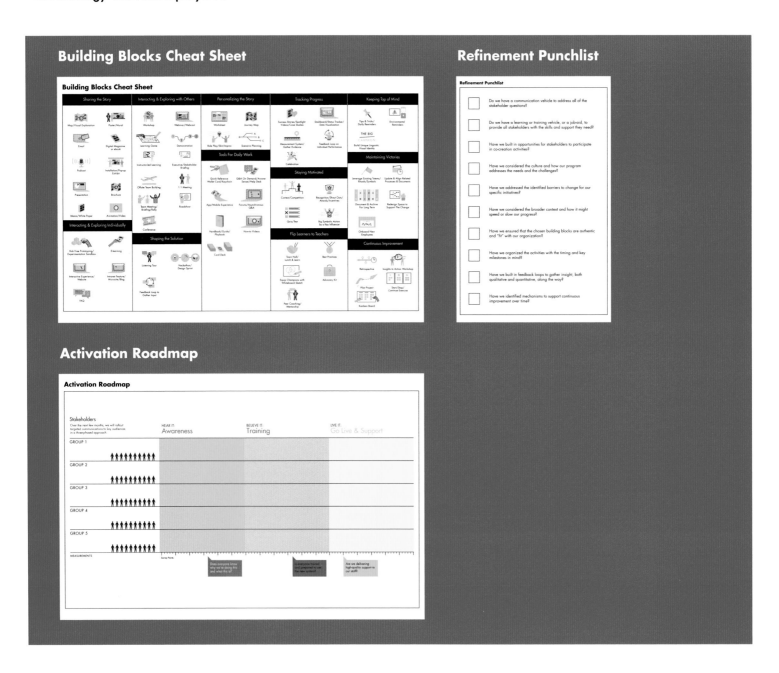

Activation Roadmap

Phase 3: Design

Chart the course ahead and prepare for known and unknown needs.

The third reason that strategies fail, very simply, is that we fail to invest in activating them. Better stated, we fail to invest in activating the people. We don't see the need to spend money or time to persuade, invite, recruit, and engage that 7 percent or more of the people we need to tip the scales in favor of successfully bringing our strategy to life.

In modern organizations, as we've learned, people have increased agency and empowerment. So we can't assume we can jump right from strategy to execution. Instead, we need to bridge the gap with communications, learning, and support to persuade and equip people to successfully move in new directions.

To do this, we need to combine our vision, insights, and recommended actions into a plan—a campaign if you will—of activities to help people bridge this gap. We need to design a strategy to activate the strategy, tailored to fit the unique needs of our people, organization, and context.

The Goal

The goal of this phase is to design the activation plan, which details specific investments to deliver information and activities to targeted stakeholders over time.

Leveraging the activation curve as a framework, we'll design this campaign in three phases:

1. **Hear It:** Communications

2. **Believe It:** Learning, development, and support

3. **Live It:** Entrench change into the organization

Our campaign will be tailored to the needs of each stakeholder group, sequencing activities in a consistent cadence to ensure each group moves up the activation curve at the pace required to meet our goals.

Once complete, the activation plan answers the needs uncovered in prior phases to provide the scope of investment required to successfully align and equip our team to execute the strategy to achieve our vision.

The Theory

Like we prepare for any expedition, we want to outline who will be on the journey, where we need them to be and by when, and what tools they'll need at each stage to succeed.

Though we have the journey itself in mind, we aren't planning the actual execution of the journey. Rather, we're planning the preparations for the journey: both how to recruit people to join us on the journey, and how to train and equip them for success.

The activation plan has three primary elements:

- **Stakeholders:** Begin by identifying key stakeholder groups. These may not represent your entire organization—rather, they are the most critical groups to get on board for success. You'll place stakeholders along the Y axis of the activation plan. You identified key stakeholder groups during the Discover phase. Start with these groups and refine them as needed during the program.

- **Milestones:** Define program and activity timing within a framework of phases and milestones. You'll place milestones along the X axis.

  #### Milestones are defined by two factors:

  » The start and end of each phase of the activation curve—Hear It, Believe It, and Live It. Specifically, when they are planned to begin and when they need to be completed.

  » The goals of the organization: What key events or driving deadlines might affect our plans or define a dependency? For example, if a major event like an annual leadership summit or a global customer conference creates a deadline for preparedness, it should be included as a milestone.

- **Building blocks:** Identify specific activities or deliverables needed by stakeholders at each step. You'll place building blocks within "swim lanes" to the right of each stakeholder, ordered by the milestones.

  Building blocks are specific activities to engage stakeholders, such as communications, learning, job aids, and events.

The activation plan considers goals from the vision map, measures for success, and insights generated in prior phases to shape a sequence of activities.

The Practice

The core of the practice of developing an effective activation plan is the selection, combination, and sequencing of a set of activities that we call the building blocks.

While no two activation plans are the same, a common underlying structure and a set of frequently used building blocks form part of the strategy activation toolkit.

LEGO bricks have fascinated me and generations of people around the globe for their simplicity of structure and complexity of possibilities—simple elemental blocks that can be combined and recombined in infinite ways. We use LEGO bricks in our work with clients at XPLANE, and the very creative firm has also been a past partner and collaborator.

Like LEGO bricks, this simple set of building blocks can be combined and recombined to create an effective activation campaign to address the needs of most organizations.

We've structured the building blocks as individual elements, but each also fits into a specific category or "use case" to help understand where best to place them.

Activation Roadmap

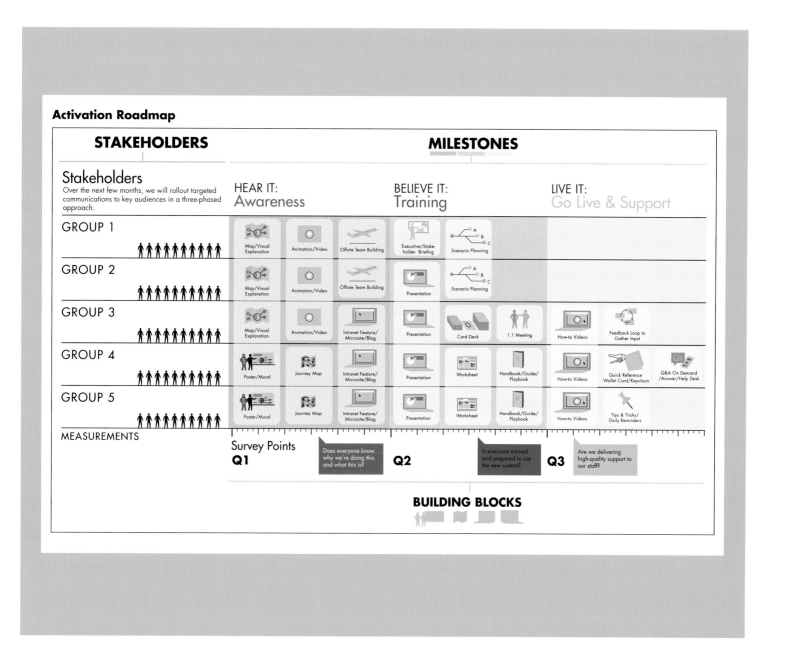

Building Blocks Cheat Sheet

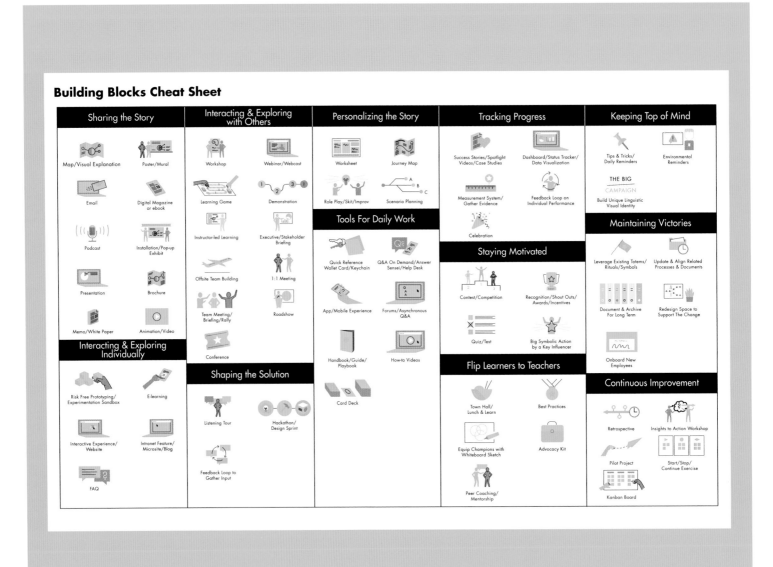

Here are twelve categories of activation activities, with typical building blocks for each:

1. Sharing the Story

To ensure that everyone understands the vision, the case for change, and the impact on individuals, we equip storytellers—leaders and change champions—with tools to tell the story consistently and confidently.

These are your primary communication tools—anchor communications to share the vision and the case for change at the highest and broadest level. Common examples include the tried-and-true PowerPoint presentation, as well as alternatives like videos, animations, and structured team meetings.

2. Interacting and Exploring Individually

We need to account for different learning styles, and many people—especially introverts—prefer to take in new information on their own. These building blocks allow people to explore new information on their own time, at their own pace, so they can develop a foundation of understanding before engaging with others on the topic.

These support your broadcast communications with a slightly deeper dive into the information. Examples include white papers, interactive websites, and playbooks.

3. Interacting and Exploring with Others

For many people, especially extroverts, learning is best done in groups. Whether through workshops, role-playing, or open discussion, include some group exploration in the program.

These enable group learning and synthesis by introducing ideas and allowing the team to discuss and engage them, leading to deeper shared understanding. Examples include group workshops, brown-bag lunches, and team learning games.

4. Shaping the Solution

Employee engagement and co-creation is vital to successful activation. We recommend including a few building blocks that allow for employees to react to the challenge by contributing solutions, resulting in the added benefit of their more likely support of solutions that they helped to create.

These are a special type of group experience—going beyond one-way communication, the goal is to have people contribute ideas and make existing ideas better. Hackathons are a great example: bring a group together with a "How might we?" prompt, and see what creative solutions result.

5. Personalizing the Story

Internalization is necessary to move up the activation curve. Include a few building blocks that allow individuals to internalize what the change means to them and their daily ways of working. One example is a worksheet for an employee to fill out about their role in a new process, or a discussion template for a manager and employee to use in a one-on-one meeting.

These can be done individually or in small groups, but in all cases, they facilitate the process of envisioning yourself doing things in a different way.

6. Tools for Daily Work

Sometimes the barrier to adoption isn't alignment with the direction, but the need for skills and support for new ways of working. What job aids or tools can be deployed to help people be successful at the point of need? Examples include signs, quick reference cards, and handbooks.

These are practical, on-the-job reference tools—something to reach for in the moment.

When deploying some new processes with the U.S. Marine Corps, for example, XPLANE developed a waterproof quick reference guide which fit neatly into a Marine's cargo pocket, at the ready when needed until the new procedures were second nature.

7. Tracking Progress

Visible results build support and momentum. How can the organization measure progress and make the results transparent to the organization?

These measurements may be quantitative, like success metrics, or qualitative, like success stories. Often, they're a combinatiaon of the two, serving to demonstrate progress, build a sense of accomplishment, and inspire others to action.

An employee-facing dashboard is a common example, perhaps shared during team meetings and town halls. These also include successful case studies and celebrations of key milestones achieved.

8. Staying Motivated

Remember, this is a journey, not a sprint—we'll need to keep people motivated with a cadence of support and reinforcement. Examples include regular "shout outs" at team meetings, a featured recognition spotlight in your internal newsletter or on social media, and periodic contests.

These should focus on two things: celebrating and recognizing successes, and building anticipation or excitement for the future.

Recognition is one of the most powerful tools a leader has to motivate behavior change. Celebrating a job well done, especially publicly, not only rewards the person who did a great job but inspires others to mimic the behavior. Creating anticipation and excitement also serves to create and sustain motivation—whether through a skills assessment or a team competition.

9. Flip Learners to Teachers

To create a movement, learners need to become the next teachers so that change can multiply and spread from within. For example, many of XPLANE's most successful programs have included an ambassador program as a core element. Engaging a cross-section of representative employees in specialized training and supporting them with tools and methods for success also equips them to spread best practices to others.

Be sure to select a few building blocks that equip people to learn new ways of working and share them with peers. Whether through actively teaching new methods, serving as a role model, or acting as a resource for co-workers, new ways of working spread more quickly in an organization when they are shared among trusted peers.

10. Keeping Top of Mind

What rituals, signposts, and flags can we use to signal what's important in this organization? How do we ensure our effort is present in everyone's environment and therefore top of mind? Examples include environmental reminders like posters, murals, video monitor content, and "tip of the week" email campaigns.

Think of these as your drip marketing campaign. After launching a big program, how do you maintain the momentum? Think of ways to build a regular cadence of reminders or support to ensure that the program remains visible.

11. Embedding Change

How do we entrench new ways of working, realign supporting systems, and build ongoing support for continued success? Think of areas that need to be reviewed or refreshed to ensure alignment, including systems, processes, and training programs. Examples include new employee onboarding materials and alignment of incentive plans to support goals.

These are all about making changes stick by ensuring that systems and processes support new ways of working.

12. Continuous Improvement

Lastly, what mechanisms can we deploy to entrench our success so we can build and improve on it every day?

One of our clients recognized as they rolled out a campaign of "tips and tricks" that their teams were innovating new best practices, so they created an intranet site where employees could document their "recipe cards" for new tips and tricks, adding to their catalog while spreading best practices across the company. This is a great example of a continuous improvement building block that you can build right away.

The last step of the activation curve is "look into the future" for a reason—we want to ensure that even as we're embedding new ways of working, we're building on our successes, identifying and sharing best practices, and envisioning improvements.

Beyond the examples here, we encourage you to think up new building blocks that will work well in your organization. Include approaches that have been proven to work—not only are they authentic to your culture, but people are also already familiar with them, lowering the barrier to adoption.

To be effective, building blocks must meet these criteria:

1. **They must answer a need identified in the Discover phase.** To quote an old design adage, "A solution should be as simple as possible but no simpler." Every building block should be there for a reason, an answer to an insight generated in the Discover phase.

    Have you addressed key stakeholder questions? Check. Have you provided the tools and training they require? Check. Have you built in activities to reward successes, measure progress, and embed progress? Check. Is there anything in our plan that doesn't directly answer a known need? Remove it.

2. **They must feel authentic and appropriate to your organization.** Not every building block is effective in every organization—some just don't fit. For example, a hackathon may be a fantastic co-creation workshop among employees of a software company—it's a familiar model and culturally aligned. But it may not be the right thing to introduce in a more conservative, security- and process-minded institution like a bank.

    Ensure that the building blocks you select—even if they are meant to stretch boundaries and be a bit disruptive—will be accepted by the organization, or the effort might backfire.

To ensure we understand why we're using each building block, we also ask these questions:

*   **Who is it targeted to?** Is this building block applicable to all stakeholders, or is it targeted at a specific group or groups of stakeholders?

    Activities aimed at more people may give us more bang for the buck, but we won't be able to target the content as tightly as we would by speaking to the wants and needs of a single audience. It's a tradeoff to keep in mind as we make our selections, especially if we are working within a tight resource budget.

*   **What is the goal?** When we use this building block with the stakeholder group, what is our desired outcome? How will we know if we're successful?

    Every building block should have a specific goal in mind. To be successful, we need to know the desired outcome for our workshop or hackathon, and how we will know if we've succeeded.

With these considerations in mind, let's select an initial set of building blocks for your activation plan. We want to provide a balance of building blocks to meet the criteria above, while ensuring that we've covered the variety of ways people learn.

To do this, let's start by selecting two building blocks from each category. This ensures that we have a representative group from each category, while forcing us to focus on the most impactful options.

With our selections made, we then want to ensure we've covered the gaps and opportunities highlighted in our insights report. Have we addressed every key communication need? Do we have learning and training for those who have highlighted a skills gap? Have we provided the right job aids to support adoption? Have we built in ways to reward success and spread best practices?

Review the insights report and refine your selections accordingly. Depending on the insights, you might choose to reinforce one category or phase. For example, in the DEI (diversity, equity, and inclusion) program we referred to earlier, we chose to invest less on communications (as most everyone was already on board) and more in learning and job aids (as people were hungry for training and support).

Now is the time to make adjustments from our strict "two per category" starting point. Which areas do we need to reinforce? Where do we not need as much investment? Which gaps do we need to close? Revise your building blocks as needed.

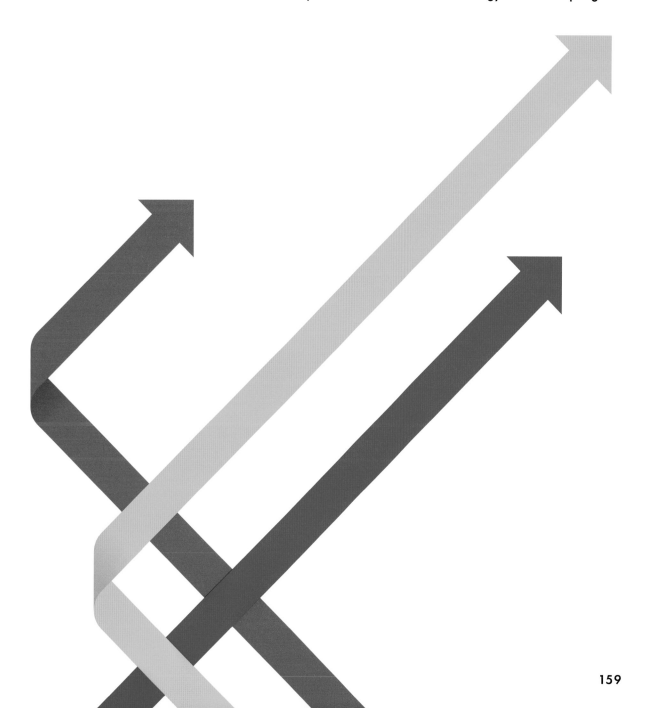

With our refined building blocks selected, we're now ready to draft our initial activation plan. For this, we'll use the Activation Plan Template:

Instructions for Use:

1. Begin by establishing the frame for your activation plan. Using the worksheet, define both axes of the template.

2. On the left, list key stakeholder groups. The order doesn't matter—it's not meant to represent a hierarchy—but it is useful for design purposes to put groups with similar needs near one another.

3. Across the bottom, identify the timeframe and key milestones that define your program goals. Are there driving deadlines to consider, like a public announcement or a planned merger? Are there milestones that might present issues or opportunities, like a company offsite or a customer conference? Place these on a timescale across the bottom, and mark goals for the endpoint of each stage.

    Note that these dates are your best guess at this point. They will be influenced by the needs of the organization, its readiness to adopt change, and the investment made in each stage. With more effort, a program can go faster; with less effort, it takes longer. In general, we assume it takes roughly three to five months to move through each stage, meaning that 80 percent of the organization has achieved that level.

4. Next, populate the activation plan by placing your building blocks into the three phases of the activation curve:

    » **Hear It:** Which building blocks are predominantly communication tools?

    » **Believe It:** Which building blocks are predominantly learning tools or job aids, or serve to convene teams to co-create new solutions?

    » **Live It:** Which building blocks reward behaviors, spread best practices, or embed new ways of working into the processes and procedures of the organization?

5. Within each phase, identify which building block is targeted at which group(s) and when it will be deployed.

    Start by arranging the building blocks in the order in which they will be rolled out. In most cases, there is a logical sequence by which activities build upon one another.

    Then, for each building block, place it in the "swim lane" of the stakeholder group it is targeted at. Many building blocks, especially in the Hear It phase, will be targeted at multiple or all groups, while others impact only one or a few stakeholder groups.

With this complete, you have your initial activation plan.

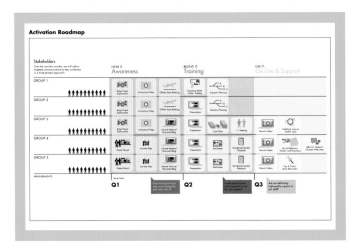

160

Activation Roadmap

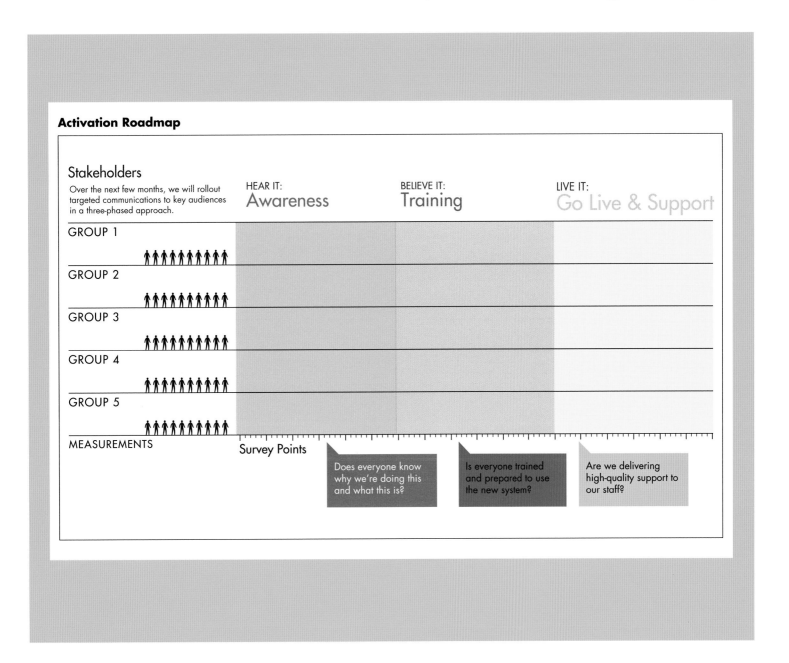

Stakeholders

Over the next few months, we will rollout targeted communications to key audiences in a three-phased approach.

HEAR IT:
Awareness

BELIEVE IT:
Training

LIVE IT:
Go Live & Support

GROUP 1

GROUP 2

GROUP 3

GROUP 4

GROUP 5

MEASUREMENTS

Survey Points

Does everyone know why we're doing this and what this is?

Is everyone trained and prepared to use the new system?

Are we delivering high-quality support to our staff?

The final step of this phase is revision, which involves weighing these considerations:

- **Identified needs:** Review your insights report and recommended actions from the Discover phase to ensure you've addressed all the prioritized needs. Better yet, engage peers or select stakeholders to review it together—it's another opportunity to engage people, which will surely reveal revisions that you may have missed.

- **Resources available:** It's a sad reality that resources—budget, staffing, time—are limited. Now's the time to review the plan with an eye towards resource requirements and availability, and to refine it to maximize the impact in the most important areas with the resources that you have.

Use this refinement punchlist to evaluate and refine your plan to meet the most important needs within your budget and resources:

If you've accommodated each item in the list, it's likely you've developed a robust activation plan. The Discover phase is complete when you have an insights-informed, resource-aligned plan to execute across your organization.

Refinement Punchlist

- [ ] Do we have a communication vehicle to address all of the stakeholder questions?

- [ ] Do we have a learning or training vehicle, or a job-aid, to provide all stakeholders with the skills and support they need?

- [ ] Have we built in opportunities for stakeholders to participate in co-creation activities?

- [ ] Have we considered the culture and how our program addresses the needs and the challenges?

- [ ] Have we addressed the identified barriers to change for our specific initiatives?

- [ ] Have we considered the broader context and how it might speed or slow our progress?

- [ ] Have we ensured that the chosen building blocks are authentic and "fit" with our organization?

- [ ] Have we organized the activities with the timing and key milestones in mind?

- [ ] Have we built in feedback loops to gather insight, both qualitative and quantitative, along the way?

- [ ] Have we identified mechanisms to support continuous improvement over time?

Governance Planning

Governance Planning

NAME OF INITIATIVE:

PURPOSE
What is the purpose of this governance program?

PROCESS
What is the process by which these people will govern this initiative?

When and how frequently will we meet?

What is our agenda?

What actions can we take?

PEOPLE
Who are the participants in this governance program?

Who is the accountable leader?

Who is the supporting team?

PERFORMANCE
How will success be measured?

Short-Term

Medium-Term

Long-Term

Measurement System

Measurement System

NAME OF INITIATIVE:

What outcomes would we see if we achieve our vision?

What qualitative measures will improve?

Resulting Dashboard: What are the top qualitative and quantitative measures we'll use to track this initiative?

What quantitative measures will improve?

Activation Plan Progress?

How will we know when everyone is aware?

How will we know when everyone is engaged?

How will we know when everyone is living it?

Action Plan: What steps do we need to take to install measurement and ensure we can collect and report this data?

Phase 4: Execute

Embark on the journey, measure progress along the way, and adapt and refine throughout.

Now comes the time to take the journey. Aware of why most strategies fail, we've taken these steps to prepare ourselves differently:

- Developed a clear vision and measures of success so everyone has line of sight to our destination, knows their roles in the journey, and will know when we've arrived.

- Engaged employees in mapping the terrain ahead and charting our course, and developed detailed plans to engage them as we move forward.

- Committed resources to activating, aligning, and equipping our team through a planned program of strategy activation.

With this work behind us, we are fully prepared to bridge the activation abyss and move forward with executing our strategy.

The Execute phase is the linkage point between strategy activation and strategy execution. The one accelerates the other, resulting in significantly greater chances of success.

The Goal

The goal of the Execute phase is to help people understand, apply, and embed new behaviors required to execute the vision, increasing the likelihood of reaching our destination.

As people understand and embrace the vision, begin to apply and internalize new ways of working, and embed these new ways as "business as usual," our strategy and vision become a reality.

However, the Execute phase isn't simply a "fire and forget" launch of our plan. It requires a continued investment in mindfully activating the strategy, and specifically a commitment to measure and monitor progress and make course corrections as we execute our activation plan.

We've planned the journey, yes, but as we embark, our role shifts from planner to guide. This is the most important role of all—keeping our party on the course, no matter what obstacles or opportunities arise.

The Theory

The Execute phase is based on a discipline called wayfinding. Drawn from navigation and orienteering, wayfinding is defined as "the process or activity of ascertaining one's position and planning and following a route."[2]

Wayfinding is an active, agile, and continuous process of sensing your current position and responding with changes as needed.

There are four phases to wayfinding:

1. **Orientation:** Determining one's location relative to nearby objects and the desired destination

2. **Route decision**: Selecting a direction and course to reach the destination

3. **Route monitoring:** Validating that the current route is still on the planned course and heading towards the destination

4. **Destination recognition:** Recognizing when the destination is reached

Let's examine how the phases of wayfinding apply to our efforts.

- **Orientation** requires us to know where we are, how far we've come, and how far we still have to go. To do this, we'll leverage the measurement system we developed in the Envision phase. By determining measures of success and putting in place a way to track and report progress, we'll be able to orient ourselves along the journey.

- **Route decision** requires a charted course, which we did initially in the Envision phase, and a structure to revise our route as needed, which we'll develop in this phase as our governance model.

- **Route monitoring** combines our measurement system and governance model to ensure a functioning process to determine when course corrections are necessary.

- **Destination recognition** incorporates our vision map and measurement system to make our arrival at the destination clear to all.

As you can see, the process of wayfinding is an active approach to staying on track, requiring a continuous investment in measuring, monitoring, and course correction.

Wayfinding is the process or activity of ascertaining one's position and planning and following a route.

The Practice

There are four steps in the Execute phase, though they should be thought of as an iterative loop rather than a linear process. The process of wayfinding is built on the concept of sensing where you are and responding with course corrections as needed, so by nature this phase will continue in a series of iterative loops until the destination is reached.

The four steps are:

1. Design the governance model.

2. Launch the program.

3. Measure progress.

4. Refine as needed.

Let's explore what's involved in each step.

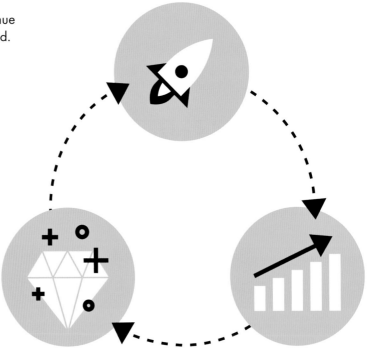

Design the Governance Model

Your governance model is the place where all the phases of wayfinding come together. This is where you set the course, orient, monitor the route, make course corrections as needed, and ultimately make the call when the destination has been reached.

The core of a good governance model is the Four Ps:

- **People.** An effective strategy activation program should include at least the following leadership roles:
  - » **A sponsor,** who leads the initiative and has enough influence to resource it properly and remove obstacles as they arise.
  - » **Initiative leaders,** who are accountable for executing the building blocks of the activation program.
  - » **An executive sponsor,** who may also be the sponsor or an executive leader to whom they report, and who ultimately advocates for and resources the program.

- **Purpose.** The purpose of a strategy activation governance model is straightforward: to execute a program to advance people in the organization up the activation curve so as to achieve the desired future state as quickly as possible. Below that are tactics, which vary from initiative to initiative, but at a minimum include measuring progress, meeting periodically to review progress and discuss course corrections, and revising the plan to adapt to circumstances as they arise.

- **Performance.** You must agree on key measures of performance used to navigate the program. What are the measures of success, how far do we expect to get by each milestone, and how will we know when we have achieved it?

  You'll need a simple dashboard and a system to collect data, so your team can see progress clearly and know where to focus its attention to keep the initiative on track. You can begin by using the measurement system developed in the Envision phase.

- **Process.** Your process is how you as a group will engage to achieve your purpose, given performance to date.

  Will you meet monthly? What is the agenda? How will the team track progress, report obstacles, and resolve issues? Who decides when and how to make course corrections?

To facilitate the design of a basic governance model, use this governance planning worksheet:

Instructions for use:

1. In the upper left quadrant, define the purpose of the governance program—typically, to ensure the successful execution of your vision.

2. In the lower left, identify the people who will be part of the governance team, including a clear and accountable leader who is empowered to make decisions and allocate resources.

3. In the upper right, describe the process the team will follow, including when they will meet, how they will work, and what actions are in their charter to take.

4. In the lower right, define the measures of performance that the team will use to track the initiative. Typically, this includes the measures from the dashboard developed as part of your measurement system in the Envision phase. Array these as short, medium, and long-term goals, if appropriate.

This is an important time to revisit the measurement system you developed in the Envision phase. With the benefit of additional discovery and the clarity from your activation plan, you may need to refine your initial measurement system.

Let's return to the measurement system worksheet:

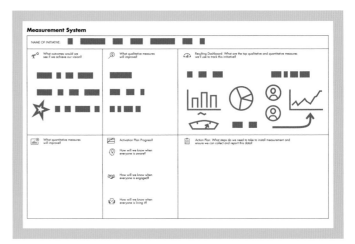

Review and refine as needed to ensure that the most important measures here are aligned with the performance expectations documented in your governance plan. Your measurement system can now serve as the dashboard for your initiative.

It's hard to overstate how important a functioning governance model and measurement system is to successful strategy activation. Far from being relics of the old way, our governance model and measurement system ensure the agile wayfinding needed to sense changes along the route and respond with course corrections to keep the program on track. As a change leader, this is where you should invest most of your time once the program is launched.

Governance Planning

NAME OF INITIATIVE:

PURPOSE
What is the purpose of this governance program?

PROCESS
What is the process by which these people will govern this initiative?

| When and how frequently will we meet? | What is our agenda? | What actions can we take? |

PEOPLE
Who are the participants in this governance program?

Who is the accountable leader?

Who is the supporting team?

PERFORMANCE
How will success be measured?

○ Short-Term ◐ Medium-Term ● Long-Term

Launch the Program

With a clear activation plan, measurement system, and governance model, we are now prepared to launch the program.

Don't expect that the program you designed will be the program you complete. This is by design. We've built the wayfinding process into our approach, which means that from launch, we'll be engaged in a cycle of measurement, refinement, relaunching with course corrections, and so on.

At each step, build in measurement and feedback loops and monitor the outcomes. That feedback is monitored through our governance model. When we sense a meaningful signal in the data, we'll respond with the necessary course correction.

Course corrections can come in many forms. There are obvious moments where something just isn't working—we hit an insurmountable obstacle or got an activity wrong—and a pivot is required. But there are also times when the measurement system tells us we're surging faster than planned and have gone farther than expected. In these cases, the appropriate course correction is to celebrate our gains, then shift planned resources to a new area that needs them more.

It's hard to say which phase of strategy activation is most important. Certainly, without a vision no journey can be launched; without discovery, your chances of successful navigation are greatly diminished; and without designing an activation plan, your team will be misaligned and unprepared. But the Execute phase is where change leaders show their true strength.

If we've set a clear vision, mapped the terrain, and properly prepared the team, then the Execute phase is a process of consistently inching closer and closer until the destination is reached. Success is cumulative and accelerated.

But the Execute phase requires commitment, focus, and will—even when others have lost theirs. Successful change leaders recognize that this phase—perhaps more than any other—requires constant attention and leadership to achieve results. Leaders serve as guides, responsible for the wayfinding required to keep the effort on track.

If leaders have a clear vision and are willing to press forward, course correct when necessary, remove obstacles, and secure resources for the next leg of the journey, the destination will eventually be reached.

The Leader's Role: Seven Best Practices for Leading Strategy Activation Programs

Perhaps you are a change practitioner, either independently or within an organization. Perhaps you are a business leader who's accountable for change and transformation programs within the scope of your team. Perhaps you're an advisor to one or both and impact change programs through your counsel.

In every case, you are a leader who is steering change programs to their successful conclusion. While you may or may not be doing the ground-floor work of leading workshops, creating initiatives, and developing the building blocks of a strategy activation program, you are still accountable for successfully implementing a strategy to achieve desired results.

As a leader, you need to be very adept at bridging the gap between strategy development (the plan of action to achieve a vision) and strategy execution (the aligned and orchestrated actions an organization takes together as a whole).

In the middle of that is strategy activation: helping each person in your organization to see the vision and the case for change, understand their role in it, and know how you'll support them in moving forward.

In our decades of leading programs and observing the leaders on our client teams who were highly successful, a few practices stand out that they all held in common.

The seven practices are:

Make it visual.

If you can't explain the vision on one page, it's not clear to you and it won't be to them. Creating a one-page visualization of your desired transformation enables you to explain the change clearly so others can see the same future you do.

Make it measurable.

The next practice is to understand the outcomes and impacts that will result if the vision is achieved. These are your measures of success—mileposts to tell you how far you've come. Without a measurement system, you'll have no idea where you are and how to lead the effort, so this is a core element of a change leader's toolkit.

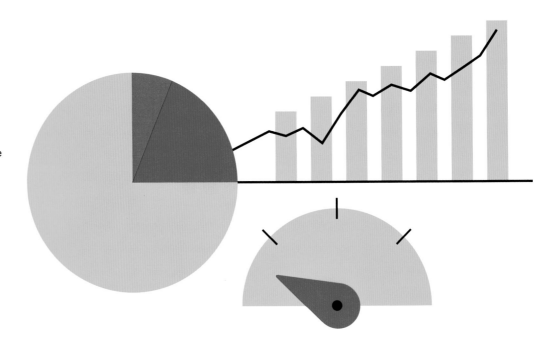

Make it people-centered.

As a leader, you'll be on the front lines of shifting your organization's approach to change management from process-driven to people-centered. Old habits die hard, and we as leaders need to help our peers see how business has changed, meaning that our approach must adapt to the needs of our living organizations and the people within them.

Make clear that the program focuses on diverse stakeholder groups across the organization, addressing each one's unique wants and needs. One size does not fit all, and the program must be shaped by the specific needs of the people involved.

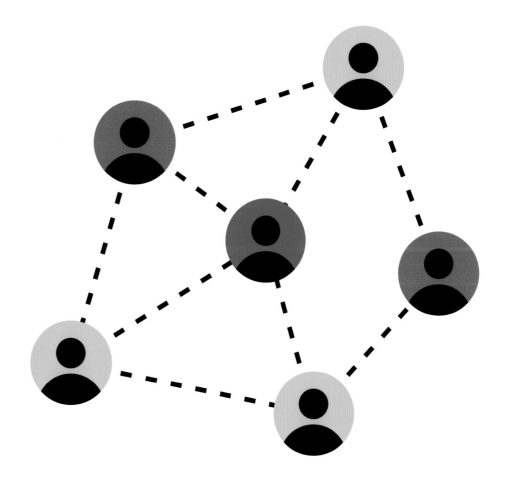

Co-create solutions.

As the work progresses, require that the stakeholders who are impacted are also engaged in the process. Ensure that representatives of each stakeholder group have a voice in defining the problem and crafting potential solutions.

We do this for two reasons. First, in a living organization, insight is embedded in the people in the organization. No consultant can uncover the full breadth of insight that lives inside an organization and its people. Remember that the smartest person in the room is the room, meaning that collective intelligence lies in the combination of perspectives. We need that to create the best outcomes.

Second, the process of co-creation accelerates change adoption. People support that which they create, and employees who are engaged in the solution are more likely to support it themselves, advocate for it to their peers, and adopt new ways of working more quickly.

Activate people.

Make the activation curve your most powerful guide to shaping your program and how you sequence and manage it. Many leaders still fall prey to the expectation that all they need to do is tell people what to do, and it will happen. That's simply not how humans are wired—especially modern workers, who have been selected and empowered to be creative, innovative, and critical thinkers.

We need to understand how people learn new information, try new ways of working, and internalize it to new embedded habits. We must invest the patience, time, and resources to bring everyone along on the journey.

Though it seems like a big investment, a well-crafted twelve-month activation program that achieves success 80 percent of the time has a much higher ROI than a traditional investment with only a 20 percent success rate.

Design in governance.

Though it may sound archaic in this discussion of change in the modern organization, a simple and agile governance model is a necessary element of a leader's toolkit. The goal is to design a model that measures, monitors, and adapts to changing circumstances as the organization advances in the journey—much like the GPS system you'd take on a road trip.

The key is to keep it simple and agile—you don't take a three-ring binder with every possible agenda on a road trip. Create a simple plan with milestones and basic contingencies. Governance enables you to keep momentum, measure progress, and realign actions as you take stock of your progress.

For leaders, the governance model is the command center—the bridge of the ship—where the vision, measurement system, initiatives, and initiative leaders all come together to chart progress and make course corrections.

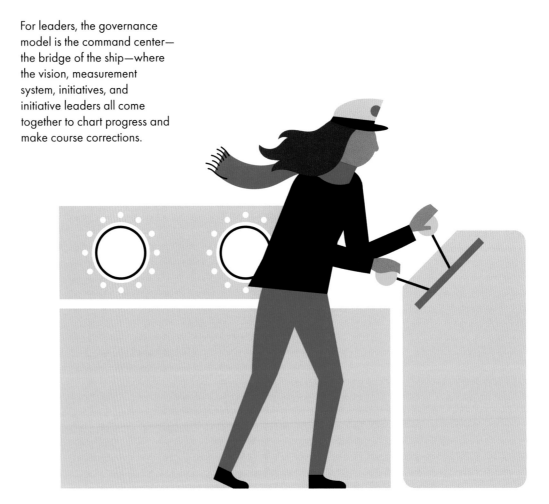

Embrace agility.

Lead your strategy activation program with flexibility, openness, and willingness to pivot in the face of new information. Remember the military adage "No plan survives first contact with the enemy?" Plan on your plan not working as you imagine, and prepare yourself to adapt to change—and your team and governance system to expect it.

New information is your friend. If you accept progress and insights generated along the journey as guidance, you will be better prepared to leverage new opportunities and mitigate new obstacles quickly. Consider "beginner's mind"—rather than stress about a setback or ignore a potential opportunity, explore all new information with curiosity to see how it might inform your next steps.

> **"**
>
> *The only thing we know about the future is that it will be different. Trying to predict the future is like trying to drive down a country road at night with no lights while looking out the back window. The best way to predict the future is to create it.*
>
> —Peter Drucker
>
> **"**

Even if you're not leading the program yourself, you can imbue it with every one of these practices. You can role-model them in meetings, you can ask probing questions to encourage others to adopt them, and you can hold your teams accountable for including them in plans.

Any of these practices can make an enormous difference in the quality of your activation program, and cumulatively, they will tip the scales to make it a success.

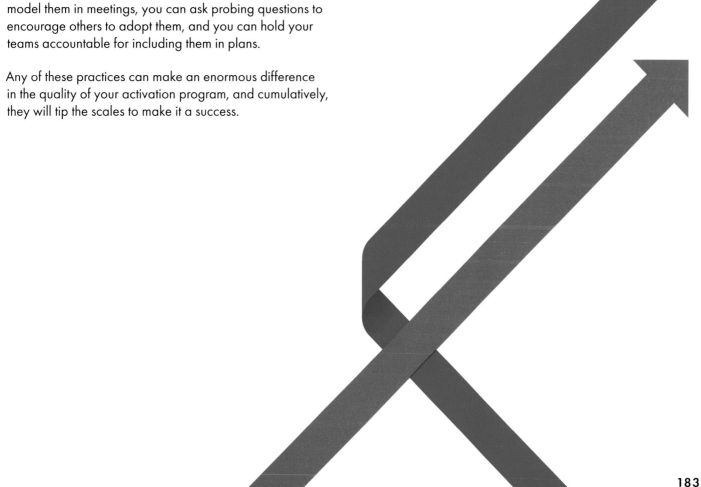

Final Word: Leading Change through People Is Your Most Powerful Capability

What will define success for leaders of the future? I believe that a leader's ability to navigate change by motivating people to achieve an organization's purpose will be the single most important driver of their impact.

All of the trends suggest a world of work that is more independent, empowered, and fragmented than the hierarchical command-and-control organizations of old. Organizations will be made up of loosely-connected, networked teams—a mix of employees, contractors, gig workers, and specialists, changing affiliations from project to project.

If we were to step back and look for a current example for this future, leadership might look less like a general commanding an army and more like a film director guiding the realization of their vision in a movie company. Think about how film companies work—the working world of the future is already taking this form: people gather around a core purpose to bring some new creative vision into the world, a team of experts are assembled into a networked organization, possibly in many compartments, "teams of teams" each with their own ways of working and different

wants and needs. Even within those teams the employment model might range from permanent employees to gig workers contributing a special bit of expertise to the overall endeavor.

While producers and the studio have leadership roles and influence, the director holds the vision and the responsibility to guide the entire organization to realize it. They do this through influence and understanding the motives of the stakeholders, and by aligning everyone around a shared vision of the outcome they are creating together.

This is the model to keep in mind as a change leader—for in this work, you are the director and the vision holder, and your chief responsibility is to lead people to achieve a shared vision.

Change is an accelerating constant. In Gartner's annual Emerging Risks survey, "pace of change" was the number one emerging risk highlighted by senior executives.[3] No prior generation has had to pivot and course-correct more frequently in response to internal and external stimuli. The ability to hold two ideas in mind at once—a steady march towards a shared vision, along with the agility and flexibility to change course throughout the journey—must be ingrained in the leader's toolkit.

A leader's ability to harness change to accelerate the achievement of purpose is the basis of their impact. It will seem like magic to some—how do they get their team there faster than anyone else? This magic can be broken down into a systemic approach to change plus the skills and capabilities to lead change through people.

Leaders can't make an impact without the organization. As with a movie company, power is now distributed across teams of teams, like a network of hubs connected by spokes. This magnifies the challenge even further, as leaders aren't always connected to each hub and sometimes must depend on hubs multiple degrees away. Hence, being able to lead with vision and activate teams to work together in the same direction is more important than ever.

This is a great opportunity for leaders. The ability to align and direct teams of teams is a force multiplier—your impact is magnified not only to those connected to you directly, but also to networks your immediate network connects to. So while the demise of the command-and-control mindset makes the challenge of change adoption greater, the investment in actively engaging and activating people around a common vision greatly magnifies the potential impact well beyond the walls of your organization.

The ability of leaders to reshape the organization to achieve a collective vision will be the core capability in the coming era—defining who gets results and who does not, and which organizations make an impact and which do not. Making change in the future will require coordination of large groups of increasingly loosely connected teams to orchestrate results together.

The only way to lead change effectively at scale is through people. It's a wonderful paradox in our technology-driven society: while more and more work is done by automation and digital transformation, humans are elevating ourselves to a collective network of creative innovators, envisioning our desired futures and leveraging the technologies and resources at our disposal to create them.

The definition of a future leader won't be the one with the best strategy, it will be the one with the best ability to execute strategy through people at scale by uniting them to achieve a shared vision together.

A leader's ability to navigate change by motivating people to achieve an organization's purpose is the single most important driver of their impact.

Endnotes

Part 1:

1. Robert S. Kaplan and David P. Norton, *The Balanced Scorecard* (Harvard Business Review Press, 1996).

2. "Size of the Consulting Market Worldwide 2011–2020," Statista Research Department, May 7, 2021, https://www.statista.com/statistics/466460/global-management-consulting-market-size-by-sector/.

3. Peter Tollman, Perry Keenan, Stéphanie Mingardon, Diana Dosik, Shaheer Rizvi, and Stephanie Hurder, "Getting Smart About Change Management," BCG, January 5, 2017, https://www.bcg.com/publications/2017/change-management-getting-smart-about-change-management.

Part 2:

1. "Women CEOs of the S&P 500," *Catalyst*, August 30, 2021, https://www.catalyst.org/research/women-ceos-of-the-sp-500/.

2. Loren Thompson, "Eisenhower's 'Military-Industrial Complex' Shrinks to 1% of Economy," Forbes.com, May 8, 2017, https://www.forbes.com/sites/lorenthompson/2017/05/08/eisenhowers-military-industrial-complex-shrinks-to-1-of-economy/.

3. Efraim Benmelech and Carola Fydman, "Military CEOs," National Bureau of Economic Research Working Paper (November, 2013).

4. Mitra Toosi, "A Century of Change: the U.S. Labor Force, 1950–2050," *Monthly Labor Review* (May 2002).

5. Klaus Schwab, "The Fourth Industrial Revolution: What It Means, How to Respond," World Economic Forum, January 14, 2016, https://www.weforum.org/agenda/2016/01/the-fourth-industrial-revolution-what-it-means-and-how-to-respond/.

6. Norman Wolfe, *The Living Organization* (Quantum Leaders Publishing, 2011).

7. "About Life Detection," NASA, https://astrobiology.nasa.gov/research/life-detection/about/.

8. SEMRush Keyword Research Tool, accessed April 21, 2021, https://www.semrush.com/.

9. Laura London, Stephanie Madner, and Dominic Skerritt, "How Many People Are Really Needed in a Transformation?" McKinsey.com, September 23, 2021, https://www.mckinsey.com/business-functions/transformation/our-insights/how-many-people-are-really-needed-in-a-transformation.

Part 3:

1. Bert Klandermans and Dirk Oegema, "Potentials, Networks, Motivations, and Barriers: Steps Towards Participation in Social Movements," *American Sociological Review*, Vol. 52, No. 4 (Aug., 1987), pp. 519–531 and "Why Social Movement Sympathizers Don't Participate: Erosion and Nonconversion of Support," *American Sociological Review*, Vol. 59, No. 5 (Oct., 1994), pp. 703–722.

2. Frederick Bird and Bill Reimer, "Participation Rates in New Religious and Para-Religious Movements," *Journal for the Scientific Study of Religion*, Vol. 21, No. 1 (Mar., 1982), pp. 1–14.

Part 4:

1. Noah Parsons, "Scientific Reasons Why You Should Present Your Data Visually," Medium, February 27, 2016, https://medium.com/lighting-out/scientific-reasons-why-you-should-present-your-data-visually-7f57dcf6110f.

2. "MIT Research—Brain Processing of Visual Information," MIT News, December 19,1996, https://news.mit.edu/1996/visualprocessing.

3. Mary C. Potter, Brad Wyble, Carl Erick Hagmann, and Emily S McCourt, "Detecting Meaning in RSVP at 13 ms Per Picture," *Attention Perception & Psychophysics*, Volume 76, No. 2 (December 2013): pp. 270–279.

4. Lynnel Burmark, "Visual Literacy: Learn to See, See to Learn" (Association for Supervision & Curriculum Development, 2002).

5. Robert Horn, "Visual Language: Global Communication for the 21st Century, (MacroVU, 1998).

6. Blaise Pascal, *Lettres Provinciales*, 1657.

Part 5:

1. Attributed to Margaret Mead in *Teaching Music through Performance in Band*, Vol. 3 (GIA, 2000), edited by Richard B. Miles, Larry Blocher, Eugene Corporon, p. 13.

2. Definition from Oxford Languages.

3. "Gartner Survey Shows Pace of Change as Top Emerging Risk Concerning Organizations in 2Q19," Gartner.com, July 24, 2019, https://www.gartner.com/en/newsroom/press-releases/2019-07-24-gartner-survey-shows-pace-of-change-as-top-emerging-r.

Index

For downloadable templates of the worksheets in this book, scan this QR code or visit **www.xplane.com/strategyactivation**

XPLANE helps leaders realize change by activating people. Whether launching a new vision activating strategy or embedding new ways of working, XPLANE helps accelerate understanding and adoption by engaging teams with communications, learning programs, and tools that will accelerate adoption and results.

Aric Wood is the CEO of global design consultancy XPLANE, where he leads the firm's Strategy Activation practice. XPLANE has developed a unique approach to leveraging human-centered design, visual thinking, and co-creation to help engage, align, and activate people to bring their strategies to life.

With over 25 years of experience working with over 100 of the Fortune 500, as well as federal and local governments, non-profit organizations, and global NGOs, Aric has a unique perspective on what it takes to successfully lead change through people in organizations of all sizes.

He has shared his experience and knowledge as an author, a keynote speaker, and a university instructor, and has served on numerous commercial and non-profit boards, including The Design Museum Foundation and the Pacific Northwest College of Arts (PNCA).

Aric previously served in leadership roles at Intuit and Epinions.com, and as a strategy consultant at Bain & Company. Aric earned a bachelor's degree in International Relations from The Johns Hopkins University and an MBA from Harvard Business School.

XPLANE helps leaders realize change by activating people. Whether launching a new vision activating strategy or embedding new ways of working, XPLANE helps accelerate understanding and adoption by engaging teams with communications, learning programs, and tools that will accelerate adoption and results.